Designer Scrapbooks
with Sandi Genovese

Designer Scrapbooks
with Sandi Genovese

Sterling Publishing Co., Inc. New York
A Sterling/Chapelle Book

Chapelle, Ltd., Inc., P.O. Box 9252, Ogden, UT 84409

Published by Sterling Publishing Co., Inc.
387 Park Avenue South, New York, NY 10016
©2005 by Sandy Genovese
Distributed in Canada by Sterling Publishing
c/o Canadian Manda Group, 165 Dufferin Street
Toronto, Ontario, Canada M6K 3H6
Distributed in Great Britain by Chrysalis Books Group PLC,
The Chrysalis Building, Bramley Road, London W10 6SP, England
Distributed in Australia by Capricorn Link (Australia) Pty. Ltd.
P. O. Box 704, Windsor, NSW 2756, Australia
Printed and Bound in the U.S.A
All Rights Reserved

Sterling ISBN 1-4027-1866-7

Space would not permit the inclusion of every decorative item
photographed for this book, nor could all of the designers be
identified. Many of these items are available by contacting:
  Ruby & Begonia, 204 25th Street, Ogden, UT 84401
  (801) 334-7829 • (888) 888-7829 Toll-free
  e-mail: ruby@rubyandbegonia.com

Every effort has been made to ensure that all information in this
book is accurate. However, due to differing conditions, tools, and
individual skills, the publisher cannot be responsible for any
injuries, losses, and/or other damages, which may result from the
use of the information in this book.

This volume is meant to stimulate decorating ideas. If readers are
unfamiliar or not proficient in a skill necessary to attempt a project,
we urge that they refer to an instructional book specifically
addressing the required technique.

Introduction

The purpose of my scrapbooking is to create projects that help me enjoy my photos and the memories they conjure. I believe that photographs are the heart of a scrapbook and as such are the focus of my projects. The embellishments are used to enhance the photos and help set the mood to re-create the memories of the events and people featured in the photos.

The scrapbooks that I create to showcase my photos are not the traditional 12"-square albums. I prefer smaller-sized albums that are themed for a particular event or occasion. Many of the scrapbooks I create are gifts for my friends and family and are intended to include photos, journaling, and mementos in unique formats like lunch pails, paint cans, and boxes as well as three-dimensional paper projects. I try to keep the layouts simple and uncluttered, but I do enjoy playing with the format of the project.

Table of Contents

chapter 1

In the beginning —
Getting from There
to Here
page 8

chapter 2

About Sandi —
Getting Personal
page 24

chapter 3

My Mom & Dad
page 44

chapter 4

My Sister, Brother &
Brother-in-law
page 52

chapter 5

My Niece &
Her Honey
page 74

chapter 6

My Friends
page 100

chapter 7

My Little Friends
page 130

Acknowledgments
page 142

Resources
page 143

Index
page 144

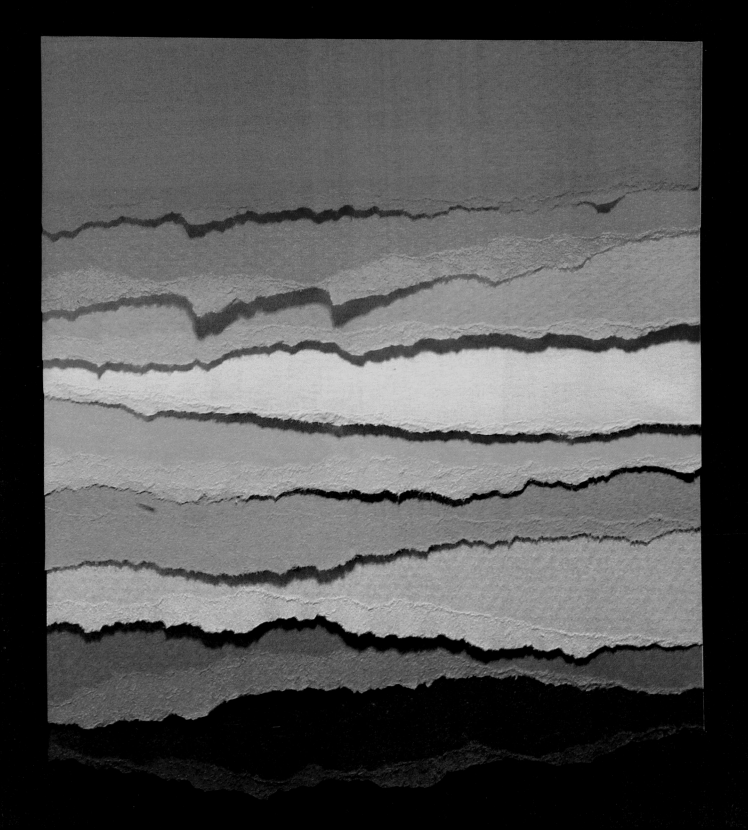

chapter 1

In the Beginning—
Getting from There to Here

I don't believe that a scrapbook is complete until the stories behind the photos are shared in the journaling. Sometimes I have so much to say, I can't squeeze it all in if I handwrite it, so I resort to the computer. I try to include something written in my own hand in each project, because I believe it is as personal and memorable as the photo itself.

I've been interviewed by various newspapers, magazines, and television hosts over the last several years, and I'm often asked when this popular hobby called scrapbooking will wane. It is my belief that as long as we all have photos, we will want to save them. As much as scrapbooking fulfills my creative urges to make something fun, beautiful, or playful, at its very core it is a way to help me remember who I am, who helped to make me the person I've become, and people I've met along the way.

Childhood

I grew up in Southern California, the middle child in a family that placed a lot of importance on the power of positive thinking and learning to think for oneself. My sister, brother, and I were taught that there is no such word as "can't," and I took it literally. I always assumed anything was possible if I was willing to work hard enough, and I believe what others see as my creativity is really just an unwillingness to give up when something doesn't work the first time. I will search for other ways to approach a problem when the obvious way doesn't work, and will oftentimes hit on an exciting new discovery in the process.

Below: Me at age three, holding Toots.

Opposite Above: Our dog Gidget.

Opposite Below: My family on Easter Sunday in 1957.

Above: Me, Mike, and Diane looking stunning at Crestline Lake, California, in 1954.

We were also encouraged to look at old things in a new way, and I can think of no better example than my father's Sunday morning pancakes. Because he was unwilling to settle for anything as ordinary as plain pancakes, he surprised us with a new concoction every Sunday morning. While the banana nut pancakes and chocolate chip pancakes weren't bad, the creamed corn pancakes were terrible, surpassed only by one Sunday's offering of green tomato pancakes (the tomatoes came from our garden). My dad's Sunday morning surprises were well known to all of our friends who stopped staying over on Saturday nights to avoid J.J.'s breakfast handiwork. You might wonder why we didn't just sleep through breakfast? Well, dad had something he called the ice-cube treatment to motivate us to get out of bed. The treatment was a can of frozen orange juice placed in the jaws

of our little dachshund Gidget, who then proceeded to slide under the covers with it and nuzzle against our legs. When we heard the freezer door open, we were up! My childhood is filled with silly stories; but the net result is a strong determination that my brother, sister, and I all possess and the belief that in our lives, anything is possible.

Graduating College & Teaching

After graduating from UC Santa Barbara, I went on to graduate school at UCLA and earned my teaching credential. Upon graduation, I accepted a position in the Newport-Mesa Unified School District where I taught for eight years. During this time, I bought a guitar at a swap meet and learned how to play it in order to motivate my fifth and sixth graders to enjoy music. As is usually the case, the teacher learned as much or more than the students, and I went on to play and sing in Laguna Beach at a lovely bed & breakfast inn named Eiler's Inn (named after the famous Laguna greeter Eiler Larson). Although I was never much good at it, my enthusiasm seemed to make up for my mediocre skills and I played there on weekends for about a year. I still find it relaxing to sit down and play the guitar.

Far Left: Dad and me at college in 1969.

Above: Sorority party 1969.

Left: Teaching at Bear Street School in 1973.

Ellison

After eight years, I left the classroom to run the curriculum lab where I designed educational games and classroom aids for the district (grades K–12). In my hunt for tools to equip the lab, I came across a die-cutting machine from a new company named Ellison. One of the owners is a talented artist who came to the lab to demonstrate their die-cutter. She took one look at the lab and hired me to freelance for her, writing and illustrating the newsletter that they mailed to customers. She also had me create the projects to be displayed in Ellison's booth at various trade shows. During my time off from the school district, I was able to demonstrate in Ellison's booth at educational trade shows; and after a year or so, I left the district to accept a full-time position with Ellison.

I thought it might be hard to give up summers and long breaks at Christmas and Easter; but I loved my new job so much, I never looked back. I started out with my drafting table in a corner of the owner's office, and over time became the senior vice president and creative director of Ellison. One of my responsibilities was to design dies and I became enamored with the concept of cutting and folding papers that would become three-dimensional when opened. My first book, titled *Memories in Minutes*, was written in 1996 and published by Ellison in 1997. In it, I explored three-dimensionality by combining it with photographs to

create scrapbook pages with movement. I wrote an article about it for a new magazine called *Creating Keepsakes*, which Carol Duvall read. One phone call and one visit later, and before I could click my red shoes three times, I was booked to do two segments on her show. Carol and her crew were so much fun to work with, they invited me back to do more segments every season. Thus began my television experience.

Above: The official ribbon-cutting at Ellison in 1996 when they moved into their current offices.

13

I was a frequent guest on another HGTV show called "Smart Solutions" and began appearing on other cable networks. I really enjoy sharing techniques with viewers and met so many great people in the process. Imagine my delight when I showed up at Universal Studios to tape a show on the Family Channel called "Home Matters," to discover that my fellow guests included Rosalyn Carter, Tim Conway, and Harvey Korman. Tim said his wife was a scrapbooker and he and Harvey did the segment with me—somebody pinch me, I must be dreaming! When I appeared on "Good Morning America," the guest list included Harrison Ford. Our meeting consisted of a nod and a brief passing in the makeup room; but still, it is an experience I won't forget.

Possibly my favorite guest appearance was on "The View." I was a guest on their 100th show and to celebrate their 100th anniversary, I created a scrapbook using the photos they sent me of all of their previous guests. I created *An Alphabetical Viewing of The View*, which began with Aretha Franklin and ended with Joan Baez, with pages in the middle that featured Burt Reynolds, Tom Hanks, Robin Leach, Mickey Mouse, and lots more.

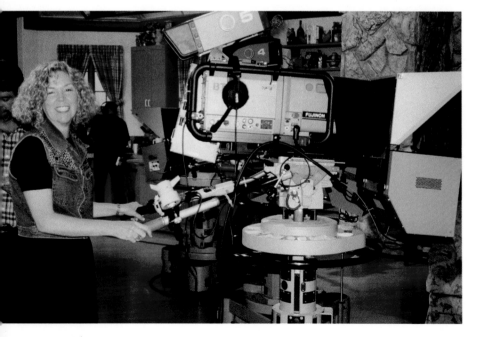

Below Left: Here I am learning about the camera on the set of "Good Morning Texas."

Below Right: On the set of the "Caroll Duvall Show" with Caroll.

They asked me to send the scrapbook out before my visit so that each host could select a page to be pretaped. During the show, as the hosts reminisced about their favorite shows, the monitor displayed the corresponding scrapbook pages, which eventually led to my interview where we talked about how viewers could use the same scrapbooking techniques at home. I was so impressed with all these ladies. I couldn't believe it when I was singled out from Diane Sawyer and other guests that day by Meredith Viera. We walked into the green room as a group and Meredith asked, "Who made that fabulous scrapbook?" and when I mumbled, "That would be me," they all gathered around to discuss the book. It was here that I realized how universal scrapbooking is and how the enjoyment of photos, journaling, and memorabilia crosses over all boundaries. These were five powerful career women with super-busy schedules, and they were as interested in scrapbooking as you and I.

Above: With Barbara Walters in the green room of "The View."

Right: With Tim Conway, and Harvey Korman on the set of "Home Matters."

15

DIY

Over the years, I continued to write books and guest on other television shows. In 2001, I was approached by the people at DIY (the Do-It-Yourself Network) to host a show on scrapbooking. I thought it would be so easy—just show up and read the teleprompter—now you're talking simple, right?

My first day shooting was on September 10, 2001, in Knoxville, Tennessee. I was trying to learn how to listen to the director in my earpiece while completely engrossed in the guest's project, all the while watching my floor director giving me cues with his hands that looked like some ancient tribal sign language. I was cursing Carol Duvall under my breath for making it look so easy and just starting to get the hang of it on my second day when the two planes crashed into the Twin Towers in New York. I realized how silly it was to fret over the details of this new endeavor. Even though guests couldn't get in (or out) and everything was crazy that week, I learned to relax, listen to my guests, and enjoy the process. Over the next six months, we taped 65 half-hour shows plus a two-hour special that aired on DIY's sister station, HGTV.

At the time of this writing, we have completed three seasons and several specials, and are getting ready to tape the fourth season. I'm still amazed at the number of wonderful people I meet and the new techniques I learn.

Opposite: In front of Scripps Corporate Headquarters where we taped my show in 2001.

Left: With Michele Gerbrandt on the set of my show in 2001.

Below Left: Shelly Gardner from Stampin' Up with me on the set of "DIY Scrapbooking."

Below Right: The set of "DIY Scrapbooking."

Mrs. Grossman's

In January of 2004, I decided to leave Ellison and join Andrea Grossman and her talented team at Mrs. Grossman's Paper Company. I have become friends with many of the people there, as well as their dogs (who come to work with their owners), and am excited to begin yet another new chapter in my career. With Mrs. Grossman's expansion from stickers to beautiful embossed papers, ribbons, and gems, I am looking forward to exploring wonderful new products in many different areas. Andrea has given me the oppurtunity to help create new products as their creative director. Part of the appeal of this company is their reputation as a leader, not a follower; and I am confident that we will stretch our wings together to create innovative new products to help support my scrapbook habit.

Nikon

Somewhere along the line, I realized that I was spending time and money on the design of a scrapbook page and neglecting the heart of each project, the photo. In my quest to learn how to take better photos, I stumbled upon Nikon cameras and have become their spokesperson. Once again, I am excited to be learning something new—the art of good photography. I have discovered that better photos make better scrapbook pages, and I'm having a ball learning how to apply the rules of good composition to my photos.

Opposite Left: With Andrea Grossman working on an ad at my drafting table in Petaluma, 2004.

Opposite Right: Spending time with Beau, Andrea's dog.

Above Left: I really enjoyed meeting people in Nikon's booth at The Great American Scrapbook Convention in Texas, 2004.

Above Right: It's always fun to meet fellow scrapbookers. At the Great American Scrapbook Convention, I signed autographs in Nikon's booth.

Studio & Home— Where It All Happens

My home and my studio are located in a beautiful coastal community in Southern California. I sacrificed size for a wonderful ocean view, which means I needed to be very organized in order to make everything fit. Nearly everything in my house and my studio does double duty: my coffee table is a large trunk that contains all of my Christmas decorations. Wicker baskets that function as end tables also hold a paper cutter and an adhesive machine.

Studio

I transformed my studio from a studio apartment into an art studio by simply hiding the shower with book shelves and building a wooden cover for the stove and sink area, creating a tall counter that is perfect for my extra-long paper cutter. Built-in shelves store sticker rolls and die-cutting equipment, while rolling files are used for storing rubber stamps, ink pads, and paper. I made it easy to select paper scraps by filing them according to color in two rolling files, one for self-adhesive papers and one for regular papers. Glass closet doors open to reveal master sheets of paper with canvas sweater organizers that loop over the closet rod with Velcro. These canvas cubbies are perfect for storing everything from 12"-square paper and vellum to adhesive cartridges and scrapbooks.

Left: I converted a studio apartment into a small but functional artists studio in 2004.

Opposite Left: A rolling file provides a work space on top and drawers filled with rubber stamps, ink pads, and various tools below.

Opposite Right: Built in shelving is handy for storing my Sizzix machine, dies, sticker rolls, and boxes of photos.

planning goes a long way; but the most difficult part was leaving some areas empty so that I would be able to add new supplies as exciting new products are introduced.

One entire wall of my studio is lined with stacking plastic drawers that allow me to see the contents inside. These handy drawers hold nearly all of my craft embellishments. Some are filled with ribbons and fibers, others with paints and ink pads, metal words, charms, wire, and everything in between. I found plastic accordion files are perfect for storing stickers, then placed inside two of the drawers.

I am now on a first-name basis with several of the sales clerks in my local container store as I spent many an hour there while planning my home office and studio. A little

Home

There's a little nook in my living room that I converted from a closet to an office. I had a desktop installed with adjustable shelves down one side and cubbies along the top that are perfect for storing envelopes in all different colors and sizes. (Since I make all of my own cards, envelopes are essential.) The desk holds my laptop computer and printer/copier/fax machine. I filled the shelves with baskets and boxes that hold everything from file folders and copier paper to photos and souvenirs. I found two wooden drawers at a home store, which I placed along the back wall of the desk. Each drawer is filled with art and office supplies, like colored pens, colored staples, stamps, buttons, and tons more. Although the drawers aren't labeled, they are numbered, and it didn't take long to memorize what goes where.

Under the desktop is a rolling file that holds my photos and other memorabilia, with additional photo storage in plastic boxes along the back. Sometimes I use my original photos in my scrapbooks, other times I use copies; and this is where all of my originals are stored—I always get double prints. When I get my film developed, I place my prints in the top box until I find time to organize them into the proper file.

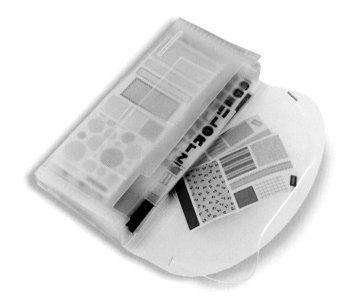

Opposite Left: My photos are placed in a photo-safe box until I have time to organize them into their proper files. My photos are filed by theme, not date.

Opposite Right: Clear accordion files are perfect for storing all of my stickers.

Above: Each accordion sticker file is also organized by theme.

Right: A closet in my home has been converted to a work area that is great for photo storage, organizing craft supplies and providing a home for my laptop computer.

chapter 2

About Sandi—Getting Personal

So often my scrapbooking is in the creation of a gift for my family and friends. I find that it's easy to forget about creating scrapbooks for myself. My own projects are similar to my gift projects in that they are vehicles to hold my personal memories and may not look like a traditional scrapbook at all. They include everything from a lunch pail filled with my elementary school memories, to an album devoted to my cat Jeepers, to a "photoless" mini-book created entirely from my New York memorabilia. Whether it's the album celebrating my surprise birthday party or the book that holds memories of my appearances on various television shows, there is nothing I enjoy more than sitting in my favorite chair with a diet soda, Jeepers snuggled against my legs, and a scrapbook in my lap. If I look to my left, I enjoy the bright colors of the flowers and greenery in my backyard; and to my right is the sparkling blue Pacific Ocean.

I don't generally go to see the same movie twice, nor read a book a second time; but there is no limit to the number of times I can browse through my scrapbooks and I enjoy it every single time!

A Pail of A+ School Memories

Elementary school was long ago for me; and in going through all of my grade-school memories, I found that they fit comfortably in this replica of an old school lunch pail. When I open the lid, I swear I smell bologna sandwiches, and it takes me back to my days at Cabrillo and Repetto Elementary Schools. Because I have more memorabilia than photos of this time in my life, I found a lunch pail (much like one that I owned) to be a perfect vehicle for my grade-school souvenirs.

I decorated the lunch pail just as I would a scrapbook page, using black chalkboard-like paper, mini wooden pencils, a metal file label, and apple stickers. I titled this "scrapbook" with a white pencil on a black tag that hangs from a beaded metal chain attached to the handle. Coincidentally, my hopscotch lager was a chain just like this one.

I shredded lined yellow notebook paper to fill the pail and cushion its contents. Then I added old report cards, my award-winning essay in the State competition, a record-store gift certificate ($1.05 for a 45 record), news clippings, a poem from our seventh grade literature magazine, and, of course, an assortment of school photos.

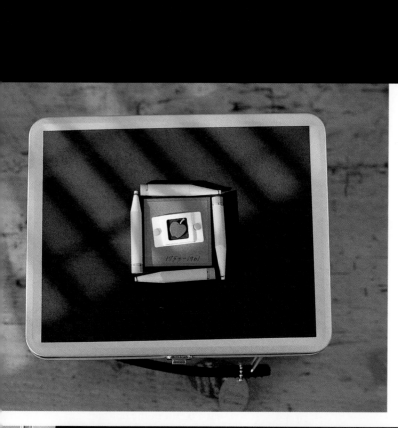

Sandi's Tip

When attaching a three-dimensional item like the faux wooden pencils onto a flat surface like the lunch pail, it is helpful to sand one side of the pencil to create a flat edge for gluing.

My journaling is handwritten on more lined yellow paper and fastened into the lid, making it the first thing you see when you open this unusual scrapbook. Even though I didn't save very many pictures from grades K–8, the wide assortment of souvenirs really helps me to relive those grammar-school days.

Elementary School

I changed schools during 3rd grade when we moved from Hawthorne to Monterey Park. I made my first trip to the principal's office during my first week at Repetto, after advising my new cafeteria friend to leave her green beans if she wanted, reasoning she had paid for them. Mr. Simon, the Principal, & I had our first of many talks & became friends.

1953–1956 Cabrillo School
1956–1961 Repetto School

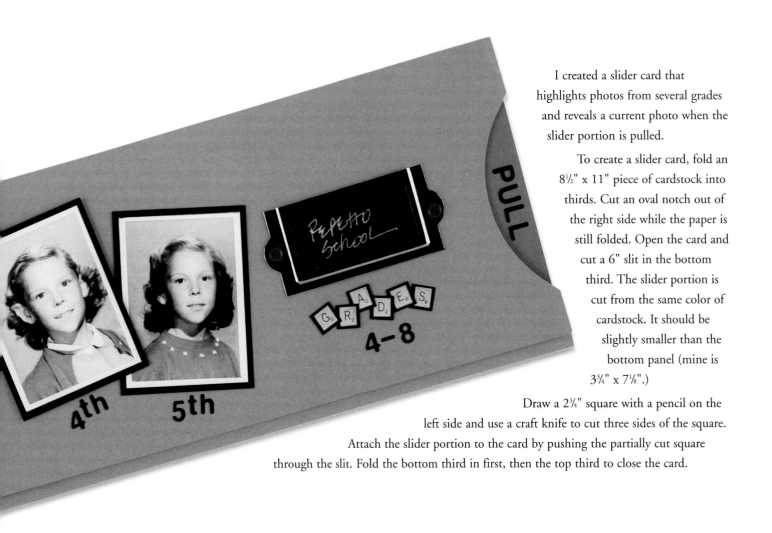

I created a slider card that highlights photos from several grades and reveals a current photo when the slider portion is pulled.

To create a slider card, fold an 8½" x 11" piece of cardstock into thirds. Cut an oval notch out of the right side while the paper is still folded. Open the card and cut a 6" slit in the bottom third. The slider portion is cut from the same color of cardstock. It should be slightly smaller than the bottom panel (mine is 3¾" x 7⅛".)

Draw a 2¾" square with a pencil on the left side and use a craft knife to cut three sides of the square. Attach the slider portion to the card by pushing the partially cut square through the slit. Fold the bottom third in first, then the top third to close the card.

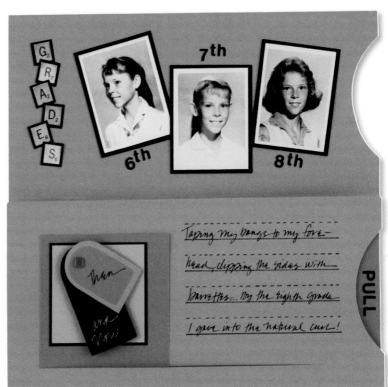

Surprise Party

I celebrated a birthday, many times, while traveling; but one time, I was greeted upon my return with a surprise party. Disposable cameras had been placed on every table, so I had tons of birthday photos. Selecting a few dozen of my favorites was all I needed to create a colorful scrapbook that highlights this special event.

The pages of the book are graduated in length and height to create a beautiful rainbow of color that can be seen before the book is even opened. The number of pages and colors can vary, but I selected 16 colors and arranged them in rainbow order. I trimmed the first two colors to 9" x 3". The next two colors are ¾" taller (9" x 3¾"). I continued to trim the remaining colors in batches of two, always ¾" taller than the preceding colors. The final two pages are 9" x 8¼". I then trimmed ¾" from the length of every other color, beginning with the first red sheet. This created a checkered type of pattern along the edge of the book. I attached die-cuts and stickers so that they extended over the tops of several pages to further enhance the fun. In order to enjoy the bright colors, I cut the black front cover short enough to allow the rainbow of colors to show. I die-cut a window in the front cover, which also provides a peek at the inside pages' birthday decor. I then trimmed a page protector to the full size of the album, punched it with the binding tool, and placed it over the top, allowing the chorus of color to show through.

Sandi's Tip

You can use fewer than 16 colors by creating a repeating pattern. For example, use red, orange, gold, and yellow, then repeat the color sequence.

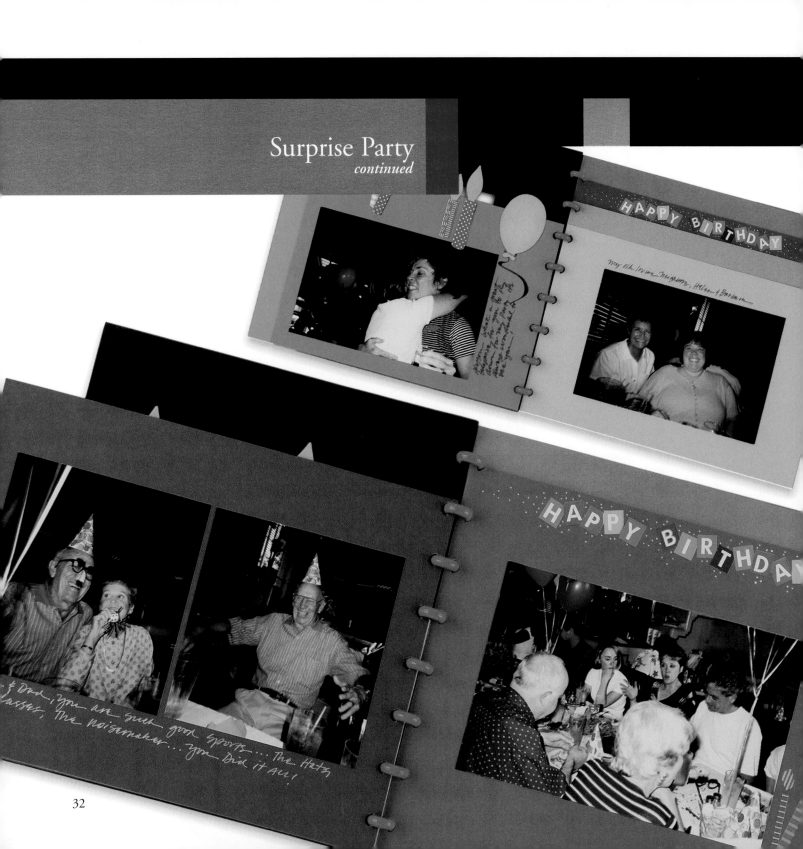

Surprise Party
continued

HAPPY BIRTHDAY

HAPPY BIRTHDAY

32

my expression says it all ... Total surprise

Media Memories

Never in my wildest dreams did I imagine that I would someday appear on television. My days as a teacher seemed to resurface and I discovered that I really enjoy sharing my creations with viewers, whether it is a scrapbook, a greeting card, home decor, or a child's craft. Although I haven't always remembered my camera or film (shame on me), I do have a collection of memories from some of my television adventures. I tried to include a photo of each guest on my show plus a few photos from my guest appearances on other shows, which resulted in tons of photos. I may still go back and add tabs to these divider pages, making it easy to locate each section.

The album where I house these photos and souvenirs is my favorite color—red, and the simple construction really appeals to me. It was easy to create title pages to divide the book into sections by decorating blank pages. Most of the journaling was done on these title pages. The photos were simply slipped into the sleeves that came in the album.

MEDIA
MEMORIES

2002

DiY

Scrapbooking

When the folks at Scripps first
called & asked me to host their
new scrapbooking series on DIY
I was unfamiliar with their
newest network. Although I had
appeared as a guest on many
TV shows I had never before
hosted a show. From my vantage
point (as a guest) it looked like
the Host just showed up & read
a teleprompter... Experienced Hosts
like Carol Duvall made it look
so easy! Listening to Joe, talking
in my ear & getting time cues
while "visiting" with
getting used

Plus 3 specials -

In order to label photos with names and dates, I cut out tags and attached them to the ring binding through the hole in the tag. As is also true in life, there is usually a way to meet your goal, as long as you're willing to be flexible and think outside the box—or album page.

Sandi's Tip

When you can't be selective with photos and need to use all of them, try this type of album where most of the decorating and journaling is done on periodic blank pages.

I have always been a big animal lover and have enjoyed owning a wonderful assortment of pets; or should I say, they have owned me. Jeepers is my five-year-old cat who is named as a tribute to the car dealership where he was born. I can be in the crankiest mood and he still makes me laugh out loud. Because he is an important part of my life, I wanted to include him in a scrapbook.

I selected an embossed cardstock in a subtle color of blue for the album pages because all of the photos look so good against it. The cover was decorated with a fabric sticker and metal buckle where I was able to loop the type of fiber that Jeepers loves to play with. I used rub-on letters directly on the cover for the title as well as on a paper strip that I fastened to the cover with a strong adhesive. Inside Jeepers' scrapbook, I have included some of his mementos like papers that he has shredded and some of his favorite ribbon toys.

Sandi's Tip

Capturing good pet photos can be a real challenge, especially with an active cat like Jeep. I found that holding a favorite toy just under the camera lens will keep his eyes focused on the camera, and creative cropping helps to eliminate background clutter like furniture legs and the limbs of my two-footed friends.

Memorable Manhattan Meals

One of my favorite cities to visit is New York; and one of the reasons why is the food—every kind imaginable, and available 24 hours a day. It seemed fitting to document a trip to New York with a gate-style scrapbook that featured some of my favorite meals, including pasta in Little Italy and my current addiction—ice cream. I forgot my camera on this trip, but found that a scrumptious scrapbook was a fun way to remember my trip, even though it was photoless.

The gate-style closure is achieved by looping metallic stickers so that they intertwine when the covers are closed. A scarlet chopstick is threaded through the loops to keep the scrapbook closed. The binding I selected is one that allows pages to be inserted and removed easily, much like Rolodex cards, without taking the book apart. I stored some of my souvenirs in page protectors that I trimmed to fit the size of the pages and punched with the binding tool. Saving souvenirs was easy, and I included everything from tea bags, wine labels, and ice-cream-bar wrappers to maps that identify a restaurant's location. I even included a note from a friend that I received while there, remembering a tasty meal. Stickers, die-cuts, and rub-on letters are used as accessories that help set the mood and theme of the scrapbook.

ARE WE there

YET?

New York City

Map

Cinnamon Stick
From an old-fashioned
recipe

STASH TEA
Earl Grey
ONE TEA BAG

A cup of tea in
the morning. The
cinnamon was the
best smelling, but the
earl grey was still
the best to drink.

In hindsight, I wish that I had included the phone number of each deli and restaurant, making it easy to check them out the next time I travel to New York.

Sandi's Tip

If you want to include wine or other self-adhesive
labels in a scrapbook ,it's helpful to keep a bottle
of un-du™ acid-free adhesive remover with you.

It's pretty Amazing how
easy it is to Find a
Haagen-Dazs Bar any-
where in the world. In
new york my Hotel was
surrounded by Delis
that Always had a
wonderful Assortment
of my Favorite A.D. Bars

Sandi ♡
I wrote this after the last dinner
we had .... I'm Soooo Slow.
I hope to see you! . I'm downstairs
in booth #1516
xoxo Jane

chapter 3

My Mom & Dad

I'd like to introduce you to my mom and dad, Jess (J.J.) and Connie. I am blessed to have parents that I would choose as friends if I met them socially. We are a very active family and my folks taught us how to play everything from tennis and golf to shuffleboard and badminton. We had a shuffleboard court painted on our carport and a badminton court (wooden strips pounded into the grass) in our backyard. Both of my parents are very athletic. Mom was a Utah State badminton champion, and both of my parents have had several holes-in-one on multiple golf courses. When we were little, my dad even cut down an old set of golf clubs and wound electrician's tape around them to make grips for us kids. Once a year, we would play golf at a pitch-and-putt course in Crestline, California. Golf is something I still enjoy with them as an adult.

We also enjoyed many family vacations in the car, and we all remember my dad's famous shortcuts. After hours of wandering hopelessly lost (trying to find a quicker route to our final destination), we would eventually stumble into some small town with a gas station. We would all cheer and mom would suggest we drive in and get directions. My dad would reply, "I'm surprised at you! That would be cheating." While we often took these unusual routes, it afforded us a unique view of the country and it instilled in us a willingness to explore new things. As an adult, I still need to remind myself that the end result is not as important as the journey it takes to get there.

Beyond the athletic fun and the vacations we enjoyed as a family, I am forever indebted to my parents for the loving and respectful example they set; and mostly for constantly praising and reminding us to think, be positive, and truly reach for the stars. There is no greater gift a parent can give a child than to build self-esteem and instill the belief that in life, truly anything is possible.

A Little about Mom & Dad

When you talk to my brother or sister or me about our family growing up, you usually hear different versions of the same event. This page, featuring photos of my parents taken more than 60 years ago, includes three tags—one for each of their children. Diane, Mike, and I each wrote a short memory on a tag. It's fun to read a bit of family history from a perspective other than my own.

Each tag slips into a slit the same width as the tag, cut into a vellum strip a little shorter than the scrapbook page. This makes it easy to remove them to read the history and memories we recorded there. The page also contains color copies of my parents' photos, matted in black, as well as the year the photos were taken, also matted in black. Three different silver heart charms dangle on black thread from the banner with my parents' names.

Another Idea

At a bridal shower or graduation party, pass advice on to a bride or new grad as well as record who was at the gathering. Each guest writes their words of wisdom on a tag and has their picture taken. After the party, create scrapbook pages, using the vellum holder as well as the tags and photos made at the party, for a lasting record of a happy time.

Naval Aircraft Training

My dad joined the Navy during World War II and ended up in the air as an airplane mechanic. I found this old photo and was delighted to discover the names of each of the men handwritten on the back. That's him, the last man on the right in the back row.

Back Row: 1. B.M. Sloat, 2. Oney D. Ives, 3. Tom Sweasy, 4. E. Solberg, 5. Charlie Hammock, 6. W.B. Selosky, 7. R.L. Mackart, 8. C.J. Salemi, 9. Stan Romanowski, 10. Jess Fuhriman; Front Row: 11. K.W. Stewart, 12. Anthony Donofrio, 13. W.H. Osborne, 14. P.B. Hudson, 15. G.W. Callison, 16. William C. Brown, 17. James A. Clark, 18. M.E Moore, 19. E.A. Kimbauer

Labeling a group photo like this can be a real challenge, so I decided to cut up a clear page protector that I positioned over the photo and held in place with a sticker strip. I numbered each person (on the page protector) with rub-on numbers and created a legend at the bottom of the page where I printed out each man's name for a simple solution that doesn't mar the original photograph.

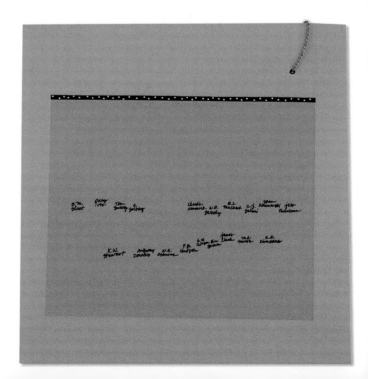

Sandi's Tip

Another way to label a group photo is to handwrite each person's name directly on a clear page protector with a permanent pen. Rub-on letters can also be used to write each name, provided there is enough room on the photo to accommodate the size of your letters.

Mother's Day Bouquet

My parents recently moved. In helping them pack, I discovered that my mom had saved many of the handmade cards that I have created for her and my dad. One thing that makes a handmade card even more special is a photograph. This Mother's Day card includes photos of my mom, her mom, and myself over the years.

The card is comprised of three strips of paper folded in half, then trimmed to create graduated pages. The pages were trimmed in ¼" increments. Because my mother is a big fan of flowers, I placed floral stickers so that they overlapped the edge of the pages. A mirror image sticker was aligned and placed on the back so that the flower can be enjoyed on the back side of the page as well as the front. The pages were stapled into the fold of a paper cover that is held closed with a ribbon tied in a bow.

Sandi's Tip

If you need to staple the middle of a book and a long-necked stapler isn't available, try this: open up the stapler and staple through the paper layers over an empty cardboard box. The pages will be stapled, but the prongs of the staple will remain open. Use the flat edge of a knife to bend the prongs closed.

Birthday Blossoms for Dad

Once my father retired, he became an avid gardener, growing everything from delicious vegetables to gorgeous roses. As a result, my mom became very adept at arranging beautiful floral bouquets, and it is rare to enter their home and not find fresh flowers in at least one room. I made this birthday card for my dad a few years back and recently discovered it in their box of treasured family memorabilia.

To create the card, I accordion-folded a long strip of white paper into thirds, then die-cut a square from the closed card. I selected three flower stickers with their mirror image counterparts to overlap each of the square window openings so that when the card is displayed it looks like the flowers are almost floating. There is plenty of room under each window to write a message, or a band of contrasting-colored paper can be wrapped around the card to act as a card cover, with lots of additional space for personal greetings.

Sandi's Tip

To prevent the sticker that is exposed in the window area from sticking to your work surface, place a leftover sticker-backing sheet, shiny side up, on the desk first.

49

Thanks for the Memories

I know that I am the luckiest girl on the planet to have such great parents, and I wanted to create a smaller scrapbook that would pay special tribute to them and thank them for some of the special and everyday things they did. While there are hundreds of "thank-worthy" things that they have done, I selected less than a dozen to highlight in this little book.

I gave the album to my folks at a family dinner and was surprised to see my dad's lips trembling with emotion as he read through the pages. It made me realize how important it is to share your precious family memories now while your family members are here to enjoy them.

Their mini book has four pages that are fastened into accordion pleats, making it quick and easy to make. Because the pages are decorated on both sides, as well as the front and back cover, the total pagination equals 10. A ribbon is looped around the folded pleats with the ribbon ends tied in a bow at the top. Inside the book, I attached a photo to each page and a tag where I explained why I was thanking them. One of my fondest memories, my dad's unusual Sunday morning pancakes, is one that I have no photos to represent, so I substituted die-cuts to tell this story, with my journaling hidden behind the folded napkin.

Sandi's Tip

Simply fan-folding a long strip of paper creates accordion pleats. I combined design with function by making the accordion-pleated spine out of a contrasting-colored paper.

chapter 4

My Sister, Brother & Brother-in-law

Growing up in the middle of an older sister and younger brother was great fun. Diane and Mike are incredibly special to me and I enjoy spending time with them every chance I get. Growing up, we hid rubber snakes in each other's beds and generally teased each other mercilessly; although Mike as the baby, was frequently the brunt of our practical jokes. Now that he lives in Denver, I don't see him as often as I'd like. However, he visits when he can and we reminisce about his famous excuse when he returned late from school one day. "The big kids made me do it," has become an inside joke in our family and was always Mike's big justification for his tardiness.

My real partner in crime was my sister Diane. We still laugh about the time we flew over the fence into the neighbor's yard when the rope swing broke with both of us on it. Every year when our cat, Tootsie, had kittens we would put them in our red wagon, wheel them around the neighborhood and give them away. Then when we were older, we had many an argument over the "borrowing" of each other's clothes. Diane was the one who took me to get my first bra, and I really missed her when she moved to Chicago to work for United Airlines. She transferred to San Francisco where she met Phil, who has become the best brother-in-law ever. Phil, an Ohio State Buckeye alum, has a quick wit that makes him great fun to be around. When I create albums for these special people, I am overwhelmed with wonderful memories of our childhood as well as our adult friendships.

The Three Amigos

I wanted to create a unique scrapbook that would chronicle my sister, my brother, and me from when Mike was just a baby (sitting on my lap) to the present. I decided to cherry-pick my family photos, spanning several decades in order to highlight the three of us over the years. This way, I can see how we have grown in the pages of one small book.

The scrapbook was made up of nine 8" squares. After folding each square multiple times, they were lined up with one-quarter of each square overlapping. The result is an album that folds into a compact little book, but stretches to 57" when fully opened.

The folding is simple: cut nine sheets of paper into 8" squares. Mountain-fold each square in half, open up and mountain-fold in half again, in the other direction. Open up and valley-fold in half on the diagonal. Open up and arrange the squares into a long line, overlapping one-fourth of each square and alternating face up and face down. Adhere the overlapping panels together.

Sandi's Tip

There are lots of different ways to organize your photos. Since I don't generally create scrapbooks that are based on chronology, I find it best to file my photos by theme. This makes it easy for me to find photos like these of Diane, Mike, and myself filed under siblings.

Sandy Memories—Photos-on-a-stick

Our family took a vacation to Crestline every year over Labor Day. So many wonderful memories, and many of them involve our days at the lake. I now live at the beach, so it seemed appropriate to display these old family memories in a sand-filled tray in my guest bathroom.

I made color copies of my old photos along with their mirror image. To create mirror image photos, I simply selected the mirror image function on the color copier or printer. Some stickers are printed with their mirror image, making it easy to add them to this three-dimensional display. Each matching pair of photos, die-cuts, or stickers has a colored wire or toothpick sandwiched between them. I added a paper umbrella to my collection and stuck them into the sand to create a three-dimensional display that I enjoy daily, all year long.

Another Idea

You can display these mirror-image types of photos, stickers, or die-cuts in plants or in five-foot-long submarine sandwiches for unique party centerpieces. Substitute bamboo skewers for toothpicks if you need them to be taller.

The Grass Is Greener

I frequently put my scrapbook supplies to good use in the creation of centerpieces for parties or just for my own enjoyment.

For springtime, I like to fill a shallow tray with wheat grass. I stick matching Easter egg stickers together, with colored wire sandwiched in the middle, and push them into the grass. Stuffed stickers, such as the bunny and the chicks, have a seam that allows me to insert a bamboo skewer into the middle to complete a truly fresh idea for springtime.

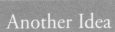

Another Idea

I have adapted this idea in so many ways for different occasions. Pumpkins, bats, and skeletons fastened to swizzle sticks are perfectly suited to top off Halloween cupcakes.

Tree-mendous Holiday Ornaments

There is no better way to mark the passage of time than with an annual photo ornament. When my family decorated our tree every year, we would literally crack up at Diane's walnut Santa, my ceramic yellow daisy and Mike's golf-ball snowman. We were each about five years old when we made them, and they looked it. As we got older our projects made us laugh even harder, hanging there next to beautiful glass balls and hand-crocheted snowflakes. I wish that we had made one every year.

Start now and create holiday ornaments that highlight a photo on the front and journaling (with the date) on the back. Be sure to remember everyone in the family, including favorite pets, and turn tree decorating into a wonderful family tradition. Select ornament die-cuts with a hole for the photo or cut a rectangular picture frame. You will need to cut doubles of each shape, allowing the photo to be wedged in the middle. Decorate each ornament with stickers and layered paper on the front, and add journaling on the back.

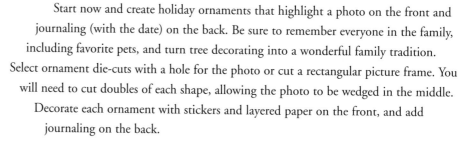

A Spoonful of Memories— Favorite Family Foods

My family marvels that my sister and I grew up in the same house, and yet she is a wonderful cook and I am not. No, that's understating it—I never learned how to cook at all! I have lived in my current home for over five years and have only used the stove twice, and then just to scramble eggs. So no one appreciates Diane's culinary skills more than I. This scrapbook is dedicated to her and includes some of her favorite recipes that she will pass on to her daughter.

The binding of this album was made with a wooden spoon and a colored hair band. Two holes were punched along the left edge of the scrapbook (the space between the holes is determined by the length of the hair band). The hair band was threaded through each hole, from the back to the front, where the spoon was slipped through each of the loops. The cover was decorated with a die-cut bowl filled with strawberries. I couldn't find strawberries that were proportionate to the bowl, so I made my own by combining tiny heart and leaf die-cuts. Each of the recipes inside is housed in envelopes, making it easy to remove in order to make each of the dishes.

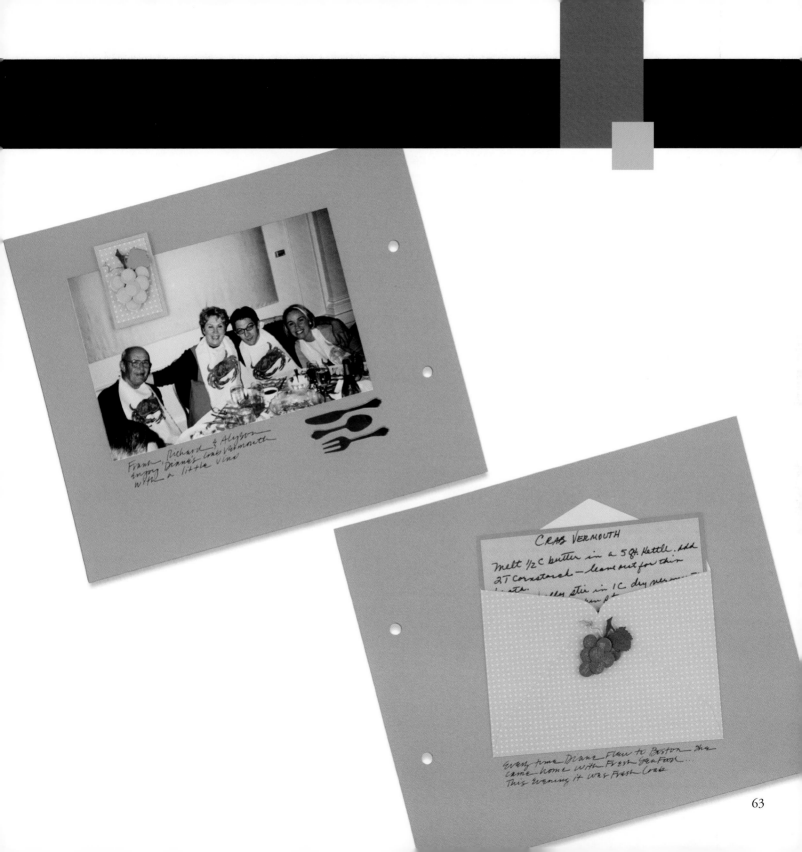

Frank, Richard & Alyson
enjoy Diane's Crab Vermouth
with a little vino

CRAB VERMOUTH

Melt 1/2 C butter in a 5 qt. Kettle. Add
2 T Cornstarch — leave out for thin
broth ... stir in 1 C dry vermouth ...

Every time Diane flew to Boston she
came home with fresh seafood ...
This evening it was fresh crab

63

Messy Crab a la Bug
2 lrg. onions, chopped, 4 garlic-minced,
½ c. butter, 4T flour, 3C milk 1C

Bug's messy crab recipe has become one
of Diane's & Phil's favorites

The Bug Sisters

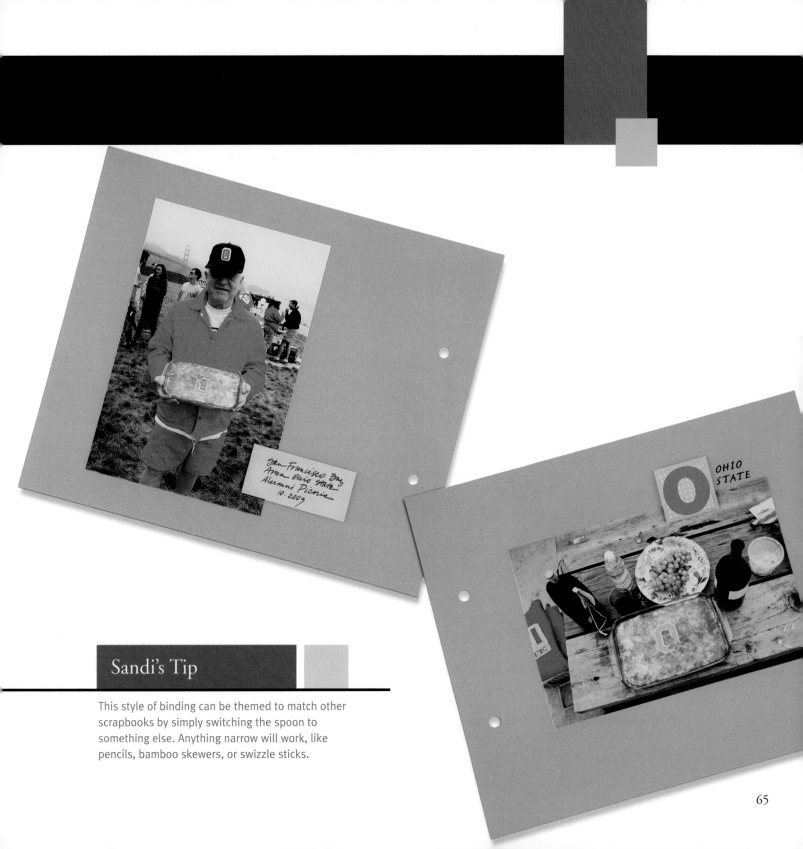

Sandi's Tip

This style of binding can be themed to match other scrapbooks by simply switching the spoon to something else. Anything narrow will work, like pencils, bamboo skewers, or swizzle sticks.

It's Elementary—Mike's School Photos

When Mike celebrated a "major" birthday, I wanted to make him a card that was special.

I found his elementary school photos, made photocopies, and stuck them in the accordion pleats of a three-dimensional card. A long strip of paper was accordion-folded, leaving a 4⅛" section at each end for the front and back cover. The number of photos you want to display determines the number of pleats. I combined metal die-cuts and metal sticker Xs and Os in two sizes to convey hugs and kisses. Each letter was matted in black before being fastened into the pleats. A college photo is featured on the cover, and a current photo of Mike and me was fastened on the inside, along with my note to him.

Sandi's Tip

It is helpful to back each photocopy with paper or cardstock for extra rigidity. The easiest way to do this is to run the photocopy through an adhesive machine and attach it to the paper backing before cutting the subject out of the photo.

A clock hangs on the wall and is referred to several times a day to check the time. It seemed like a good place to highlight some of my favorite photos. I selected old photos of Diane, Mike, and myself as children to represent 3, 6, 9, and 12 on the clock. A larger photo of us as adults is featured in the center to conceal the clockworks. Clock kits are inexpensive and come with the parts ready to be assembled into a working clock in minutes (pun intended). All you need to do is select a photo that is large enough to conceal the clockworks, then position the hands, washers, and screws.

The clock can be mounted onto decorated chipboard; but I chose to mount mine with self-adhesive magnets to a circular magnet board, which I purchased at a container store. The photos and embellishments that represent the numbers on the clock are also backed with a self-adhesive magnet. I simply placed a battery in the clockworks and the clock started ticking.

Another Idea

I created another clock that is fastened to my fridge in the same way (with magnets). I used dominoes to represent each number (i.e. twelve o'clock is the double-six domino, one o'clock is the zero-one domino, etc.). Each domino was cut from flexible magnet sheets with a paper cutter, then holes were punched with a ¼" hole punch.

67

Birthday Memories Are Popping Up—Phil's Birthday

My brother-in-law has always appreciated the gifts I have made for him over the years. This is a pop-up card that I created to celebrate his birthday. A birthday seemed like the perfect time to reflect back on years past, so I included old photos as well as a recent one. I also included his initials and birthday-themed embellishments on the pop-up tabs.

I cut pop-up cards from a series of brightly colored papers and attached them, fronts to backs, to create a mini book. Each pop-up tab was covered with a cropped photo, a birthday sticker, or a die-cut. The cover has a ¼" spine to accommodate the thickness of the book, with a narrow band that slides over the book to hold it closed. I made a three-dimensional party favor to decorate the cover, using a thin wire sandwiched between two layers of paper. This allowed me to roll the paper strip to imitate a real party blower.

Sandi's Tip

Position the photo or embellishment that is intended to go on the pop-up tab, then close the card to make sure it won't stick out beyond the card pages before you stick it to the pop-up tab. If the photo is too tall, try reducing it on a photocopier.

you've changed
A BIT
over the years

we have all changed a bit... or more

you have celebrated quite a few of these

70

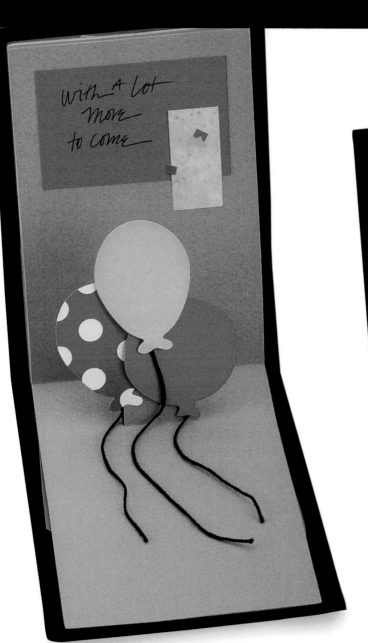

with a lot
more
to come

You're such a
Party
Animal
Have a
great one!

For the Parents—
Wedding Mini Book

Although my sister and brother-in-law have lots of photos from Alyson (their daughter) and Richard's wedding, I thought it would be fun to make them a simple accordion-folded-paper presentation that features five of my favorites.

Once I accordion-folded the paper and die-cut a square window, I simply placed a color copy of the photo behind each window, then lined the back with one long strip of contrasting-colored paper. To complete this special card, I folded paper around the closed card and embellished the front with a dramatic wedding photo and rub-on word. When the paper band is slipped off, the card can stand up to display Alyson and Richard's wedding photos in a more casual and fun way.

The picture at left shows the front of the card and the back of the band where I added the journaling.

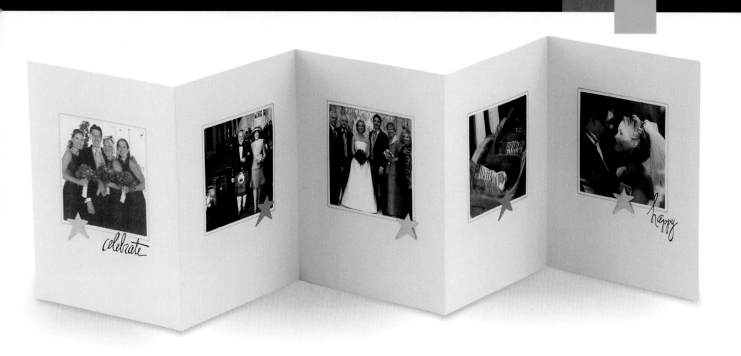

Sandi's Tip

My journaling is created in a separate square of paper that is fastened to the colored band, making it easy to do over if I'm not happy with my first attempt. Whenever you are journaling in your own hand, it's helpful to write on separate sheets that are attached last, to make it easy to redo if necessary.

chapter 5

My Niece & Her Honey

Perhaps because I don't have children, I am especially close to my sister's daughter, Alyson. Diane worked for an airline; so Alyson was able to fly for free, which made it easy for her to come visit her Aunt Sam (my family all call me Sam) all by herself when she was still a youngster. Living in Spain during her junior year in college left her fluent in Spanish and fueled a desire to travel abroad. She is currently an investigator and travels both for business and pleasure.

I had a hard time imagining a man who would be good enough for Alyson, but when she brought her friend Richard around, I knew they were a good fit. He designed her engagement ring, proposed to her in New Zealand, and took her to Bali for their honeymoon, which is all very romantic. However, when I saw how he looked at her and how great they were together, I knew they were going to be a good team.

When Alyson and Richard were married, their best man brought a horrible flu bug over with him from England. Alyson caught it a few days before the wedding, but her maid of honor was affected on the wedding day and fainted during the ceremony. Next to succumb was Richard's mom, who never made it through the reception. During the reception Richard contracted the dreaded flu and he alternated between the dance floor and the bathroom all night. I was so impressed with both Alyson and Richard and how they took it all in stride, helped everyone to feel better, and went on to have a wonderful honeymoon. They are two of my favorite people in the whole world.

Making the Grade—
Classroom Memories

Alyson attended a private school that required a school uniform until she went to high school. My sister kept Alyson's school photos as well as the pages where Alyson had written her school information each year. It's almost as much fun to note the differences in her printing/handwriting from year to year as it is to enjoy her photo each year.

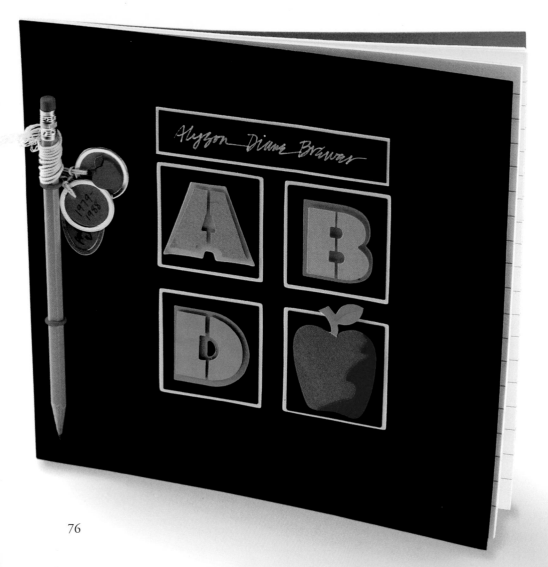

The album that I created to hold Alyson's school photos uses a hair band and pencil binding to establish the theme of the book. School information was written on the tags that are wound around the top of the pencil. Alyson's initials were matted and placed inside squares that are fastened to the cover along with an apple to complete the square. Inside the book, I occasionally placed lined notebook pages for journaling among the plain pages to evoke memories of school.

back to School

St. Matthews

ALyson DiANE
BrEweR
1979 – 1987

GRaDe ONE

SAINT
MATTHEWS
SCHOOL
SAN MATEO
CALIFORNIA
1980-'81
GRADE ONE
MS CONNOLLEY
PRINCIPAL

Bottom row
2nd from right

Age: 7
Name of School:
Date Entered:
City: San Mateo
State:

• Pets: Dinah
Farrah
Activities: tap
Ballet, Dance
• Sports: swinging
on rings
I want to be:
Artist

xAdE FoUR

ST. MAT THEW'S SCHOOL SAN MATEO CALIFORNIA 1983-84

Bottom Row 2nd From right

Teacher's Name:
Friends: Cathy, Jen,
Nicole, Catherine,
Priscilla
Pets: Dinah Panda

Favorite Subjects: History
Activities, Hobbies, Clubs:
Storus
Sing, Stickers.

City
Date En
Name
Age:
Nar

NoTE:
Sticker collecting
Was ALL the RAGE...
Even SPECIAL
Notebooks For
Storing them

GRAde SiX

ST. MATTHEW'S
SCHOOL
SAN MATEO
CALIFORNIA
1985 - '86
MRS. RUTLEDGE
6TH GRADE
CAROL FERRER
HEAD OF SCHOOL

BoTTom RoW
3rd FromRight

NoTE:
• ALYSon hAs
become ALLi
• DAViD (your
horSe) hAs
EnTErED the
PicTure

Sandi's Tip

When a scrapbook has the same elements to be
displayed on each page, create a formula for each
double-page spread that is simply repeated. It
creates a feeling of continuity and makes assembly
super quick.

Glowing Memories—Photo Candles

I saw photo candles in a book and decided to try making them as a gift for my niece and her new husband. I experimented with several different ways to fasten the photo to the candle, but I had the greatest success with an adhesive machine.

I ran a copy of the photo through the adhesive machine, removed the backing and stuck the photo onto the candle. I also added ribbon and sticker strips for additional hold, as well as other embellishments, decorating the candles much like I would a scrapbook page. The date was stamped with a date stamp I purchased at an office supply store. Straight pins with colored heads were put to good use fastening papers to the candles and as a decorative element as well.

Another Idea

Cover a matchbox with coordinating fabric stickers, paper, and a metal buckle for the final touch to this personal gift.

Engaging Photos-in-a-box

Richard is British and he met a photographer from New Zealand in a local San Francisco pub. The photographer has become their friend, and the engagement photos he took of Alyson and Richard are awesome.

I created a box to hold the photos with a band that slides off in order to allow the box to be opened. The box bottom and top were both cut to the same size, 7" x 8⅞". With a ruler and bone folder, I creased all four sides of the box bottom at 1⅜". I then cut a triangle wedge out of each corner where the sides met. This process was repeated for the box top, except that the paper was scored at 1¼" because the box top must be slightly larger than the box bottom.

This resulted in a box that is 4¼" x 6¼" when assembled, which is perfect for holding 4" x 6" photos. See the assembled box on page 74. The first card was cut to match the size of the photo mats and was decorated just like a scrapbook page with a cropped photo and rub-on letters. The engagement photos were each matted, leaving room for Alyson and Richard to write on the back.

Sandi's Tip

Set the first page apart from the rest by cropping one of the photos slightly and fastening it along one edge of the photo mat instead of in the center. Create textured background paper by decorating the deep red cardstock with a lighter shade of red hearts. Drape some of the hearts off of the edges for a more natural look.

Save the Date Fridge Photos

Save-the-date cards have become very popular. They certainly make it easier, for people traveling some distance, to book flights and hotels in advance of their upcoming trip to attend a celebration. Even though this isn't the card that was eventually sent, it's still a fun idea.

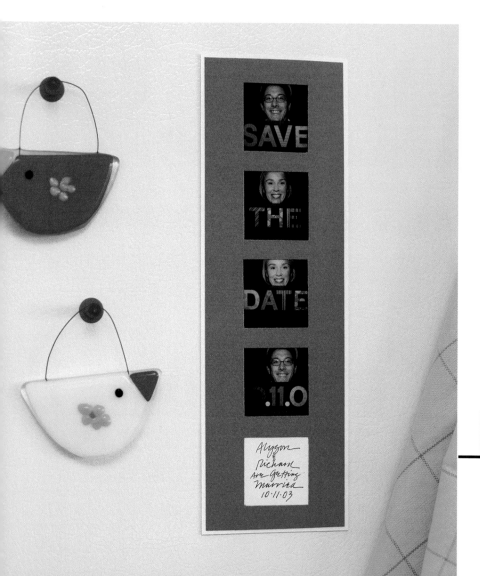

For this card, I made four signs to visually convey my message. I sent them to Alyson and Richard, who took them to a photo booth and held one sign for each photo. The photos came out in a square, so I cut them apart and arranged them in order behind a filmstrip cut from red paper. I cut an extra window to announce the special event and restate the date; a necessity since I made the last sign too long and part of the date is cut off in the photos.

Once the original is complete, it is easy to make multiple color copies—one for each invited guest. Place a piece of self-adhesive magnet behind each photo strip and slip them into envelopes to be mailed to each guest. When the card arrives, the photo strip can be placed on a refrigerator or metal filing cabinet for a unique reminder of the upcoming event.

Sandi's Tip

It's smart to do a test run—holding up blank paper strips—when using a photo booth, in order to avoid making the signs too large to fit in the photo.

SAVE
THE
DATE
.11.0

Alyson
&
Richard
Are Getting
Married
10·11·03

Wedding Keepsake Box

When my niece told me she was getting married, I volunteered to create the paper pieces for this special event. This included her Save-the-Date Card, wedding Invitation, wedding Program, and a wedding Favor/Thank-you for each guest.

I found a leather box in the same color as her bridesmaid dresses to hold all of these paper pieces, with room for additional wedding keepsakes as well. The lid has an opening for a special photo of the wedding couple, and they have it displayed in their living room.

The creation of the paper wedding ingredients took a good bit of time, and many family members pitched in to help. I was delighted to be part of their special day.

I printed and matted the information on cream cardstock, and die-cut the date out of three different papers. I handwrote "Save the Date" in gold and dropped in the loose numbers, leaving it up to the invited guest to assemble into the correct date. The card and numbers showed through a vellum envelope that was sealed with a matted gold heart.

Save the Date

October 11, 2003
for the wedding of
Alyson Brewer and Richard Hay
Cheers!

We look forward to seeing you there
Travel and accommodation details can be found
at our wedding website, www.weddingchannel.com

10 11 2003

Wedding Keepsake Box—
Invitation

I created a custom die to cut out the wedding invitation. Some die manufacturers have a custom die department that makes it easy for you to send in your invitation design to have made into a custom die. The resulting die can cut and score your invitations when placed in a die-cutting machine. Once folded, I fastened the matted wedding invitation onto the card with a gauzy paper folded over the top. Ribbon was placed under the matted invitation and held the gauze layers closed. The invitation featured a pocket at the bottom that held wedding information on separate cards in graduated heights. The reply card and envelope were also tucked into this pocket, with only the envelope flap visible over the pocket.

Sandi's Tip

When creating multiples of the same project like the wedding invitations, programs, and favors, it's faster to perform one step to all of the pieces, then the next step, rather than completing one piece from start to finish.

Directions: Reception
Directions: Church
Hotels

I printed the wedding ceremony information onto two sheets of cardstock that I cut into 12 individual tags. The tags were stacked and fastened together with a gold ball chain, then inserted into a crayon-style box that was labeled with the couple's wedding date.

Wedding Keepsake Box— Favor

Alyson and Richard opted to donate money to the Alzheimer's Association in lieu of a gift box of candy or almonds. The heart card is what I created to explain this to each guest and to thank them for coming. The card was standing on their plate at the wedding reception.

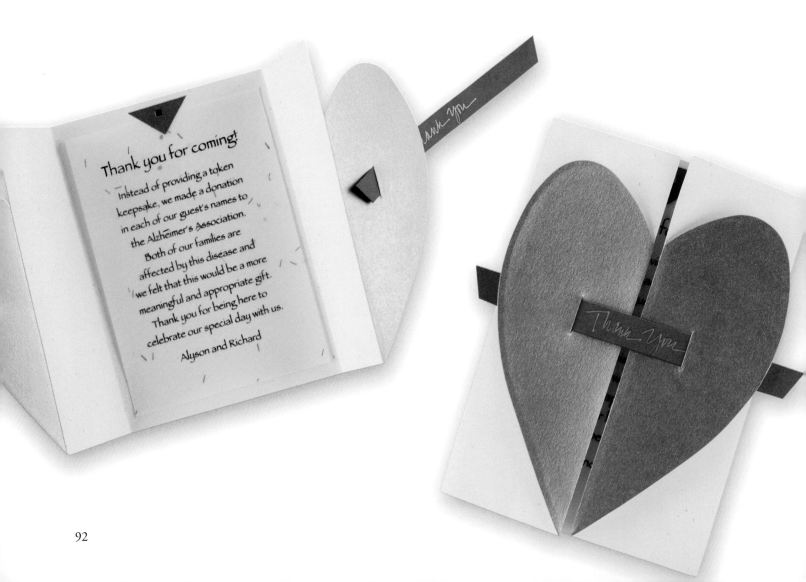

Thank you for coming!

Instead of providing a token keepsake, we made a donation in each of our guest's names to the Alzheimer's Association.
Both of our families are affected by this disease and we felt that this would be a more meaningful and appropriate gift.
Thank you for being here to celebrate our special day with us.

Alyson and Richard

A Honeymoon to Remember

Because I travel so much, I have accumulated a lot of frequent flyer miles. I was able to convert some of them into airline tickets for Alyson and Richard's honeymoon to Bali. They had some problems with their camera, and many of the photos they took are tinged with blue and lack clarity; but that won't prevent them from using the photos as a springboard to remember the great time they had.

I decorated the black cover with gold metallic sticker strips and red paper strips as the backdrop for the title block. I punched five holes along the left edge and laced a metallic ribbon through the holes, starting at the bottom and resulting in a knot at the top. I hung mini tags from the ribbon binding with matching fiber.

A Honeymoon to Remember
continued

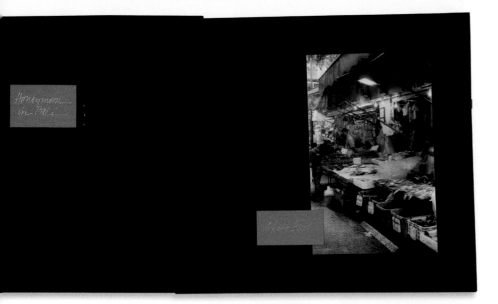

The inside pages are the same black as the covers. I used minimal decorations in the book to leave room for Alyson and Richard to add their thoughts on the pages. I created embellishments that carried the red and gold colors from the cover throughout the book.

I sandwiched a red paper clip between matching gold stickers with a wire band that encircles the gold sticker. I added a red heart sticker and then a lacquer that dries clear over the top to add some sparkle and shine to this special book.

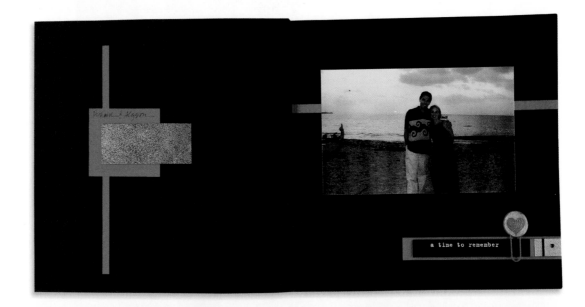

Sandi's Tip

A floss threader is the perfect tool for threading ribbon and fibers through the binding holes quickly and easily.

The Sky's the Limit— Skydiving

I remember roller-skating with Alyson when she was little. She was so cautious. I can't figure out what happened, but somewhere between childhood and adulthood she developed a thirst for extreme sports: bungee jumping in Europe and skydiving in Monterey, to name a few. This little album features her skydiving adventures with a journaling card slipped into a pocket on every layout allowing plenty of room for her to talk about her hair-raising (literally) experience.

Trim paper to desired size. Fold the paper into fourths lengthwise and thirds widthwise, creating 12 squares. Cut along the horizontal lines, leaving the last square intact at each end. Begin at one end and accordion-fold along the fold lines. When you get to an end, fold under and continue accordion-folding. The end result is a book with 12 pages. Because all of the pages are double sheets, except the first and last page, they are perfect for cutting pockets to hold journaling. Cut a slit in every other page and fasten each double sheet together around the perimeter, leaving room in the middle to insert the journaling card. Create a cover from a contrasting color and decorate it with a sticker strip, rub-on letters, and a handwritten title.

Sept. '03
Sky Diving

Monterey, California

To Alyson —
You truly love the thrill
& adventure of trying new
things... It's just
of the many things
I admire about you.

1

September 2003 —
1st time skydiving!
I finally took the
plunge! I had been
wanting to try it
for close to 10 years
but couldn't find
a partner in crime
to go with... until
now!

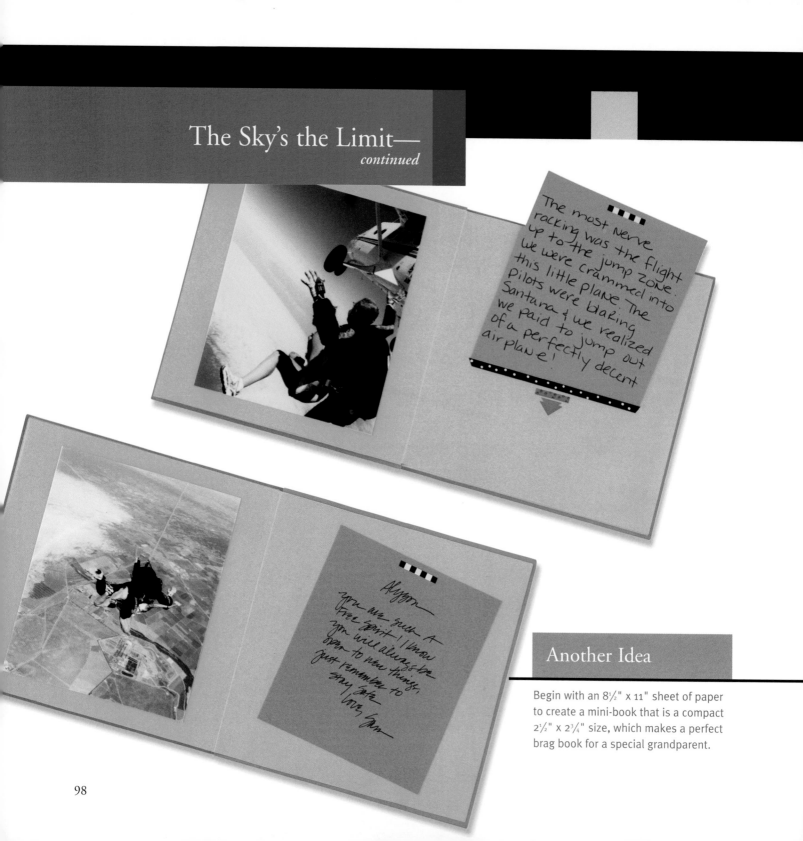

The most nerve racking was the flight up to the jump zone. We were crammed into this little plane. The pilots were blaring Santana & we realized we paid to jump out of a perfectly decent airplane!

Alyssa—
You are such a free spirit! I know you will always be open to new things, just remember to stay safe.
Love, Sam

Another Idea

Begin with an 8½" x 11" sheet of paper to create a mini-book that is a compact 2½" x 2¾" size, which makes a perfect brag book for a special grandparent.

We could not have asked for better weather. It was such a warm and sunny day I was able to wear shorts! We could see for miles up and down the Monterey coastline!

It was so incredible! The sensation was undescribable and not at all what I had expected! It was nothing like losing your stomach on a ROLLER COASTER!

chapter 6

My Friends

The fact that this is the longest chapter in the book tells you a little bit about how many great friends are a part of my life. It takes a while to handmake a special album or other photo project for friends, but it gives me so much pleasure to see their delight in receiving such a personal gift. Creating a scrapbook as a gift for someone else is truly a labor of love with the lion's share of the enjoyment going to the creator. The entire time I am creating each project, I am flooded with memories that are tied to those particular photos and the friends that are featured. Sometimes the photos are shared with me after the event, like Kristy's (my executive producer at DIY) baseball diorama of her children and her husband playing ball. Other times, I was lucky enough to be part of the special event, as in the photo wall collage of Neil and Tara (the son and daughter-in-law of a good friend) when we visited them during Neil's spring training in Florida.

A gift scrapbook can be presented complete with photos attached and blank panels left for journaling by the album's recipient. For friends who would like to finish the book on their own, present the scrapbook with a decorated cover and the first few pages complete. Include a page protector that holds the additional parts and pieces. Some people just want a little help getting started, while others get their enjoyment from browsing through the completed album rather than helping to create it.

Field of Dreams Baseball Diorama

I made this photo diorama for my friend Kristy. When she showed me her photos, they included her boys playing baseball plus a picture of her husband playing baseball when he was their age. Two generations of sports fans deserved a special presentation.

This diorama was created from four layers of paper, with each layer embellished with baseball-themed die-cuts, stickers, and photos. The project's three-dimensionality was achieved by staggering the length of each layer, with the shortest in front and the longest in back. The size of each layer was based on the size of the photos, but each layer is approximately ½" to 1" longer than the preceding layer.

Fun in the Sun Diorama

The front layer has a window cutout and the back layer is a solid piece of paper. A hole was punched in all four corners of the diorama front and back, and in the bottom corners of the two middle layers. A colored snap fastens all four layers together, creating the arc that makes the diorama stand up.

Dioramas can be created for any theme. Summer photos really come alive when cropped and displayed in a hot summer diorama.

Snow Business Diorama

Combine winter die-cuts and
punches with cropped winter
photos for a really cool diorama.

Florida Photo Wall Art

You can borrow the photos from your scrapbook to decorate your wall. A good friend of mine has a son who was a major league baseball player. His spring training was in Florida and it was a treat to visit with him and his wife. This wall art collage is a way of sharing some of the photos from our trip in a unique way.

Each of the sections is made up of three-dimensional squares or rectangles cut from foam-core board and glued together to make this collage. Blank structures like these are available preassembled and ready to decorate; or using a craft knife, simply cut your own. It is best to begin by creating a pattern. Cut paper into squares and rectangles and arrange them until you find a pleasing arrangement. Use these as patterns to cut squares and rectangles from foam-core board. Make the project three-dimensional by cutting additional foam-core pieces and assembling them into boxes. With a glue gun, adhere the boxes together. Create the boxes in several different depths to create wonderful dimension in the completed project. Glue the completed boxes together and decorate.

Sandi's Tip

I have also successfully created a photo wall collage by assembling store-bought box bottoms and lids. Nesting boxes in multiple colors are readily available in container stores and result in a multicolored surface that is ready for decorating with photos and other scrapbook embellishments.

Hanging Out with Photos—
Vellum Room Divider

Once I successfully color-copied my photos onto vellum there was no stopping me. I experimented with tons of uses for these translucent photo cousins. One of my favorites is a combination of vellum photos, vellum stickers, and large vellum die-cuts hanging from a folded strip. It is such fun to create a hanging display for a birthday, surprising the birthday girl by hanging it in the doorway to her room.

I cut a 5"-wide strip of paper to match the width of the doorway and folded it in half horizontally. I taped lengths of clear fishing line inside the folded strip and began sticking vellum photos and colored vellum circles onto the clear line, sandwiching the clear line in the middle of matching pairs of vellum stickers and die-cuts. I stopped when I reached the height of the room's occupant, so her head just brushed against the bottom circles. I decorated the paper strip with vellum stickers that spelled out my birthday wishes.

Sandi's Tip

The challenge when working with vellum that isn't a sticker is how to conceal the adhesive. I prefer to run vellum sheets through an adhesive machine. When the adhesive covers the entire surface it seems to disappear.

Heartfelt Thank-you Card

Because I am blessed with wonderful friends and family who always remember me with thoughtful gifts and favors, I'm constantly in need of special thank-you cards. This one is surprisingly easy to make.

I accordion-folded a long strip of paper and die-cut a square out of the folded stack. I then stuck vellum heart stickers together with thread sandwiched in the middle. Finally, I suspended the hanging hearts over the square openings with coordinating square vellum stickers. To prevent the strings from tangling, I wrapped a band of coordinating paper around the card, fastened it in the back, and embellished it with an embossed tag.

Sandi's Tip

I usually trim the paper, score the fold lines, and die-cut the square out of several colors of paper, keeping the extras in reserve until I need to make another card. This card format can be adapted to any theme by simply changing the color of the paper and the stickers.

Magnetic Bookmarks

I learned to read before I started school and have always loved it. I can spend hours wandering the aisles of a bookstore, and I find that I frequently give books as gifts.

There is no better way to personalize a book than with a magnetic bookmark. The bookmark can include a photo or not, and can be decorated to match the theme of the book.

Create magnetic bookmarks by folding a strip of paper in half. Leave the rectangle shape as is or cut out a shape leaving the fold at the top intact. The key is in small magnetic strips fastened to both of the insides of the folded paper shape. The magnets will clamp together onto the pages of the book to mark your place—a gift your friends are sure to treasure.

Food bookmarks are perfect for all types of cookbooks and can be easily created with a watermelon die and paper that is cut on the fold. Die-cut the green half circle leaving the fold line intact at the top. Add lighter green strips to mimic a watermelon rind. Die-cut the red portion, then place it over the green and mark the seed holes. Remove the red portion and color a swatch of black with a marker before fastening the red over the green. Add the self-adhesive magnet strips inside to complete the bookmark.

It's easy to convert your favorite stickers into a bookmark by adhering them to either side of the top of a folded paper and trimming around the sticker shape, leaving the top fold intact. A beautiful sticker lays the foundation for a bookmark that is perfectly suited to clip onto the pages of your favorite baby or gift book.

Punch a square out of a folded strip of paper to feature a friend's photo from their yearly Christmas card. Decorate with gold metal sticker strips and a Christmas garland sticker. Write the year with a white or silver pen, add the magnet strips inside and then clip the photo bookmark onto a gift book for a truly personal holiday gift.

It's in the Can—Home Remodel

If you have ever remodeled an older home or bought a new home, you know that the choices seem endless and the process can be daunting. Friends of mine renovated an older '50s-style tract house into a beautiful Mediterranean-looking home.

A paint can seemed like the perfect place to store carpet squares, flooring, tile, paint chips, fabric swatches, and other home improvement souvenirs. Each one is labeled on the back side, indicating the room where it was used with themed stickers and die-cuts added for decoration.

I decorated the exterior of the can with leftover wallpaper, die-cuts and rub-on numbers. I hung a small screwdriver from the handle to facilitate opening the can.

I documented the makeover with before and after photos that I attached to accordion-folded cardstock, then added it to the contents of the can. It was easy to label the backs of the carpet and wood flooring samples with the rooms in which they were used.

BEdRooM

Living Room Pillows

dining room

Enjoy your "OLD" Home Sandi

Sandi's Tip

Because the paint can is made of metal, you can attach embellishments to it easily with self-adhesive magnets (readily available at a hardware store).

Noteworthy Note Cards

One of my favorite gifts that I like to make and give to friends and family is a small stack of stationery or note cards. I made these for Andrea, a good friend and mentor who happens to be a heart collector. The first batch I made for her was purple and red and she seemed to enjoy them so much, she mentioned that she was hoarding them so as not to run out. Because she is a wonderful correspondent to all of her friends, I realized I needed to keep her stocked with these simple note cards.

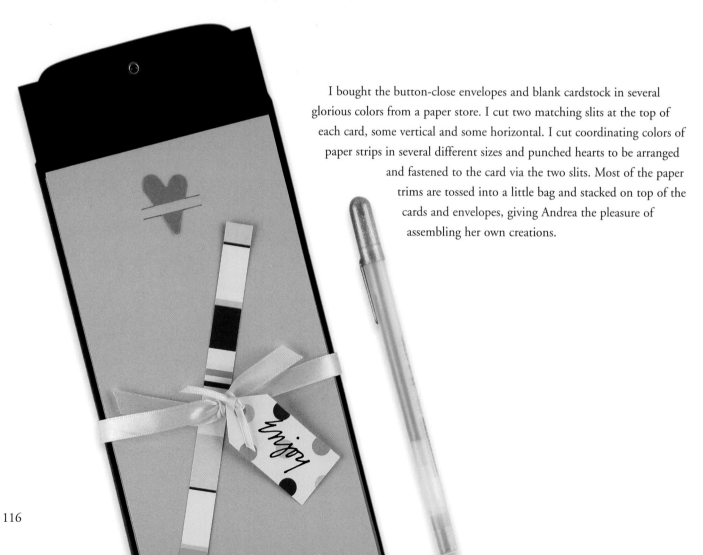

I bought the button-close envelopes and blank cardstock in several glorious colors from a paper store. I cut two matching slits at the top of each card, some vertical and some horizontal. I cut coordinating colors of paper strips in several different sizes and punched hearts to be arranged and fastened to the card via the two slits. Most of the paper trims are tossed into a little bag and stacked on top of the cards and envelopes, giving Andrea the pleasure of assembling her own creations.

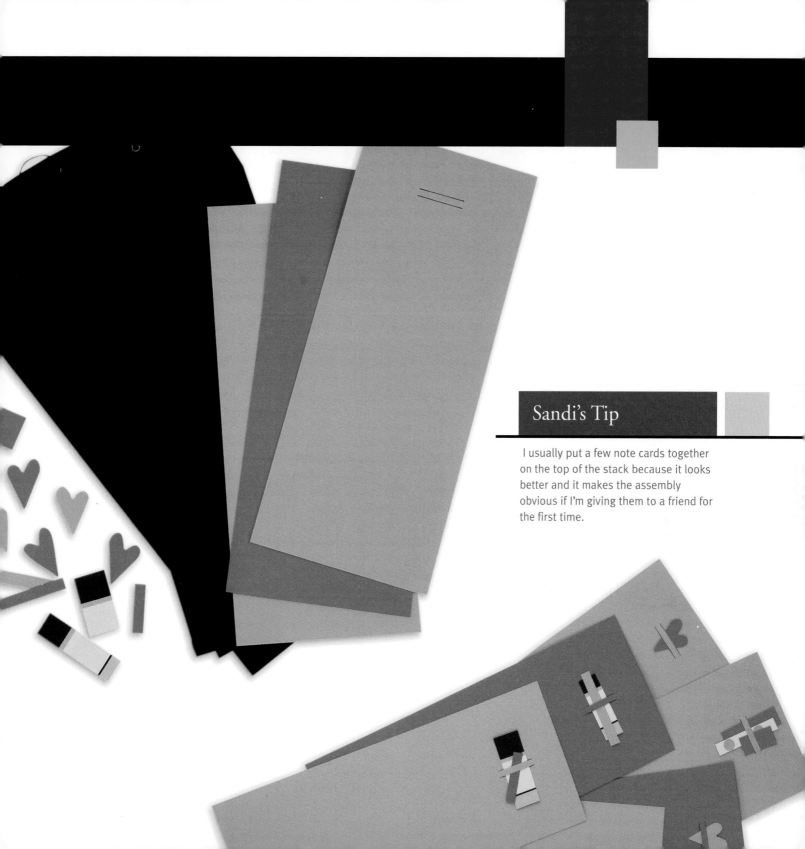

Sandi's Tip

I usually put a few note cards together
on the top of the stack because it looks
better and it makes the assembly
obvious if I'm giving them to a friend for
the first time.

The Lovely Lindsay Baby Book

Stacy, who is the senior producer on "DIY Scrapbooking," became pregnant with her second baby during our third season. She almost made it all the way through the season before giving birth to the lovely Lindsay. She has become a good friend in the three years we have been taping the show, and I wanted to make something special for her new baby girl.

I selected a pack of refill page protectors for an 8"-square album and bound them together with ribbon and a front and back cover made from doubled sheets of embossed cardstock. The cover and first few pages are decorated simply with stickers and yellow vellum that was torn into strips and cut into various-sized circles for polka-dotted pages. I have included Lindsay's photo and baby announcement plus a page protector full of additional coordinating supplies in hopes of making it easy for Stacy to complete the book as she takes more photos of her precious little one.

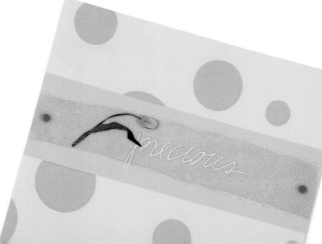

Lindsay Reece Levy

Brad, Stacy and Kathleen
welcome their new addition

June 2, 2004
11:39am

6 lbs. 7 oz.

18 inches

oh
joy

Sandi's Tip

I've discovered that two holes are not enough for pages this size. To prevent the pages from shifting, punch an extra hole in the middle and lace the ribbon through each end and back up through the middle before tying into a knot, then a bow.

There's a New Baby in the Nest—Nesting Boxes

I truly enjoy presenting a gift in a unique or special way, and have had friends complain that the gift wrap is sometimes better than the gift! Nesting boxes are easy to make and are perfect to hold a baby gift for a new mom. Decorate the lid of one box with a photo of the new baby and embellish other boxes just as you would a scrapbook page, leaving room inside the final box for baby booties, a rattle, or other small baby gift. Once the gift is opened, the boxes become a beautiful place to store baby keepsakes.

Each box is folded from a square of paper and is 1" smaller than the previous one. The box lid is ½" larger than the box bottom. This formula makes it simple to make a series of nesting boxes in any size to fit a particular need. Boxes that are created from embossed cardstock like these need the lid to be ½" larger than the bottom to accommodate the thickness of the

cardstock. The box dimensions are as follows: Large box lid is 12"-square and bottom is 11½"-square; medium box lid is 11"-square and bottom is 10½"-square; small box lid is 10"-square and bottom is 9½"-square. Draw an X from corner to corner of each square. Fold each point to center then unfold. Fold each point in again, reaching to crease closest opposite corner, then unfolding. Fold again, this time to the crease closest the corner you're working with. Angle your square to a diamond, and snip two parallel cuts along the first fold lines from center line at both the left and right of diamond, stopping at the innermost fold line. Fold the bottom point up to center and fasten with double stick tape. Fold next crease up and swing in the arms. Repeat at the top. Bring in left side point so that arms are captured underneath and fasten with double-stick tape. Repeat with right side to complete box.

Thinking of You Card

It's difficult to remember the last time I gave a store-bought card to a friend or family member. I don't always have the time to spend with them that I'd like, so I try to make up for it in a small way with handmade cards for special and everyday occasions.

I created this card from a long strip of rose-colored paper and accordion-folded it into five sections. I die-cut a square window out of the closed card, then attached embossed tag stickers so that they overlapped the window openings. A matching tag sticker was fastened to the back side of each tag, making the card reversible with tags showing on both sides. Many of the tags were decorated with rose stickers and some were raised with foam adhesive. The middle tags have thread sandwiched in between the two layers, making it possible to hang it over the middle window opening. A matching band of rose paper was folded around the card and fastened in the back to act as a card cover that simply slides off to reveal the card.

Sandi's Tip

When making a folded band that slides over the card, it is helpful to do it last in order to accommodate any thickness that is created by the embellishments inside the card.

Vacation Gift Album

A friend of mine takes such good photographs that she has become my "lending library" of photographs for some of my television projects. Many of her photos feature her children, so it seemed fitting for my thanks to her to take the form of a book of her trip to Laguna Beach with her kids.

I cut the ends of the first several pages into graduated lengths and decorated each end with vellum sticker strips. I attached vacation-themed stickers as tabs over the vellum sticker strips, with the mirror-image sticker on the back. Each page features a photo with minimal information and periodic sections of journaling on vellum papers.

Sandi's Tip

A vellum pocket is easy to make and perfect for holding vacation memorabilia like airline tickets and baggage tags. Cut a cardboard square the size of the desired pocket to act as a guide. Cut the vellum ½" larger and fold the vellum around the sides and bottom of the square. Cut a "V" shaped notch out of each bottom corner and fold around the square. Remove the square and use the ½" tabs to fasten the pocket to the page.

Wonderful Wedding Guest Book

One of the production assistants on my show met her future husband while we were taping the second season. During the taping of the third season, they were married and I wanted to make something for their special day. When I discovered she hadn't yet bought a guest book, I decided to make her one.

I began with a preembossed album that is post-bound, making it easy to add pages that have been personalized with Derek's and Karrie's names printed on the computer. I printed their names as well as the signature lines on sheets of cream-colored cardstock. I trimmed the pages to the correct size after running them through the printer and added them to the front of the book. Some of the blank pages remain, allowing Karrie to add photos, taken at the bridal shower and wedding, to her guest book. The cover and first page are embellished with a pearlized felt heart and a vellum leaf that I recycled from a gift card.

celebrate love

now and forever

Guests

Derek & Karrie

Guests

Derek & Karrie

happily

ever

after

Sandi's Tip

It's easiest to run heavier cardstock through a printer or color-copy machine, using the hand-feeder tray.

It's in the Cards—
Christmas Cards Past

All of my life I have enjoyed making cards for my friends and family members. Somehow this trend transferred to the holidays and I began creating and handmaking a Christmas card for everyone. The first one was over 20 years ago. I hand-decorated the lid from potato salad containers that I got free from the deli. I punched holes before shrinking them in the oven and turning them into hanging holiday ornaments, and my holiday tradition was born. Every year since, I have handmade Christmas cards (although one year I made Groundhog's Day cards instead, when I couldn't meet my holiday deadline). An organized person would start early, but I am always frantic to finish in time for the cards to arrive before December 25th. My fascination with paper folding and three-dimensionality is apparent when you look at two of my cards from Christmases past.

These cards can be mailed flat, then assembled by the card recipient to create a three-dimensional display.

The cubes are made from a simple box die-cut. If you do not have a similar die-cut, purchase small jewelry gift boxes like these at craft stores. Decorate the boxes on all sides to deliver your best wishes of the season to friends and family.

The tree is comprised of two green triangles, each one with a slit that interlocks and forms a tree. To create the dangling stars, I sandwiched thread between two stickers and hung them from the spiral. I added smaller holographic star stickers to the message written on the rings of the spiral.

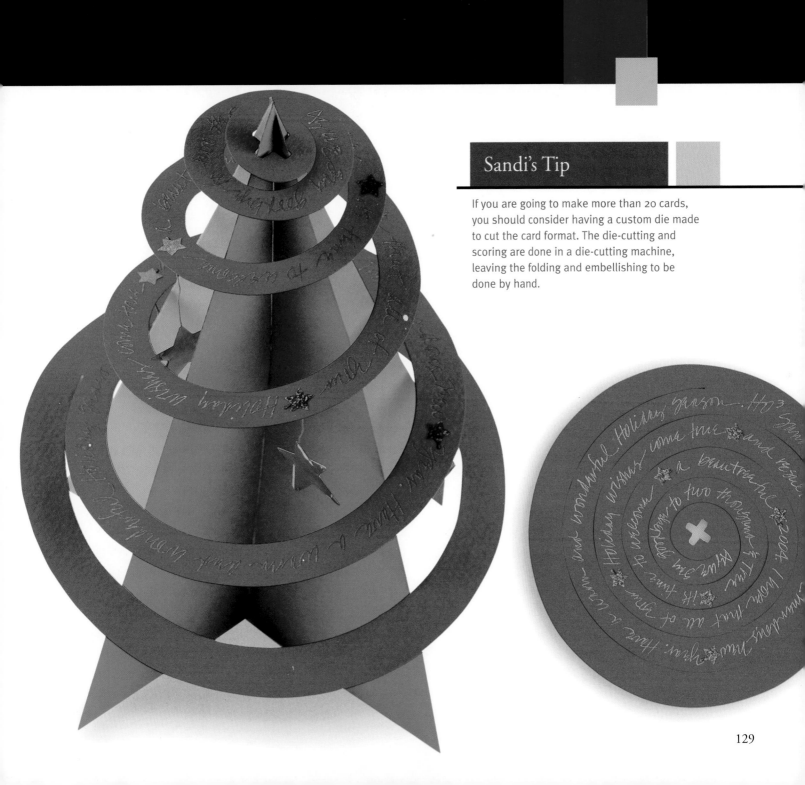

Sandi's Tip

If you are going to make more than 20 cards, you should consider having a custom die made to cut the card format. The die-cutting and scoring are done in a die-cutting machine, leaving the folding and embellishing to be done by hand.

chapter 7

My Little Friends

It's important for kids to have a scrapbook or two of their own. It doesn't need to be fancy or big, in fact smaller books are probably easier for smaller hands. It is so much fun to surprise a special child in your life with their own little album filled with photos of events and people that are special to them—including pictures of them, of course. An added benefit is the self-esteem that is built when a mini book is created that focuses on photos of the child. What could make you feel more special than a book devoted entirely to you? Mini books that feature birthday parties, Halloween, soccer games, and favorite pets are perfect for sharing with the little friends in your life.

A New Twist on Binding—Twist Ties

There are few things that make a child feel as special as a mini book that is devoted entirely to him. I enjoy making pint-sized books for the pint-sized hands of my little friends. Because family albums are usually treated with special care, these "album-ettes" are meant to be "kid-friendly" and should be very simple to make with color copies of photos and inexpensive supplies. These books are intended for kids to sleep with under their pillows, take to school for sharing, or any old thing their little hearts desire.

We have taped a few DIY specials at Kristy's house where I have had a chance to meet her wonderful family. I created these books for her two sons, Sam and Jake. To begin yours, cut colored paper to the desired size and punch holes along the left edge with a ¼" hole punch.

To create customized twist ties for bindings, place thin-gauge wire inside strips of fabric stickers that are then folded closed before being laced through the binding holes and twisted. The inside pages are nothing more than colored photocopies matted on colored paper with occasional printed journaling.

Sandi's Tip

Packages of refill album pages or refill page protectors are inexpensive and perfect for the inside pages of children's mini books. They eliminate the need to trim the paper to size and punch holes except for the front and back cover. They are available in a wide variety of sizes: 6"-square, 5" x 7", 8"-square for example.

Stretch Your Memories— Rubber-band Books

Scrapbooking is a great activity for the family, and rubber-band books are perfect for children because the supplies are inexpensive and the creation time is minimal. These little books can be made for them or with them or both!

Simply trim paper into strips slightly wider than the rubber band, fold in the middle, and slide the rubber band into position. The mini book covers are decorated very minimally with a single photo, die-cut or trio of circle stickers that I converted into balloons by adding black strings. Some of the cover designs are matted and attached, while the balloons are overlapping the edge of a square window that I punched out. Make color photocopies of photos and add embellishments that suit your fancy to complete the inside pages of a book that is very kid-friendly.

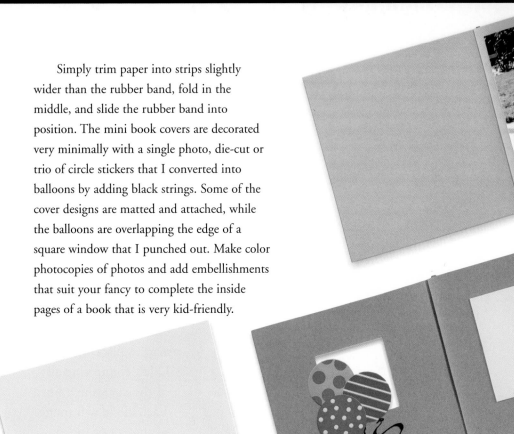

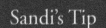

135

Snappy Photos—Snap Bindings

A little book that highlights photos of a special dog named Beau is the perfect size to give to a child who loves him. This easy-to-make mini book features circles held together with plastic snaps.

Decorate each circle, leaving space to punch two holes directly opposite each other. Once the cropped photos and embellishments have been added, select a complementary colored snap to place in the holes, connecting all of the circles in a line. Each circle will rotate so that all of the circles align into one stack, making this book the perfect size for a pocket or pocketbook.

FUN

Beau

play

Sandi's Tip

Colored brads can be substituted for the snaps, but be sure to punch the holes away from the edge of the circles to avoid seeing the prongs stick out from the back. If you have wire snips, you can also trim the ends of the prongs to keep them safely hidden behind the circles.

Sneak-a-peek Mini Book— Sticker Binding

A mini book that I created for Orry and Allie, the children of a friend of mine, incorporates a number of kid-friendly features. Each page is a bright color with a different-shaped window that can be opened to see the photos inside. The final window reveals a pop-up card with a dangling heart inside.

This book is made up of a series of six 6"-square cards (12" x 6" when opened up). Use a craft knife to cut a different-shaped window opening from each card front, leaving the window flap attached along one side so that it can be opened like a shutter. Glue the photos behind each window opening. Lay the cards in a long line, overlapping each window front to the back of the next card, then fasten them together to make a chain of cards. Accordion-fold the chain into a book. Wrap 14"-long sticker strips, cut from a sticker roll, around the first and second pages, tucking the stickers up against the middle fold of the card. Continue to bind the accordion folds into book pages by repeating this with a new sticker strip around the third and fourth pages and a final sticker strip for the fifth and sixth pages. Attach sticker tabs to each window flap to make it easier to open them in order to view the photo inside.

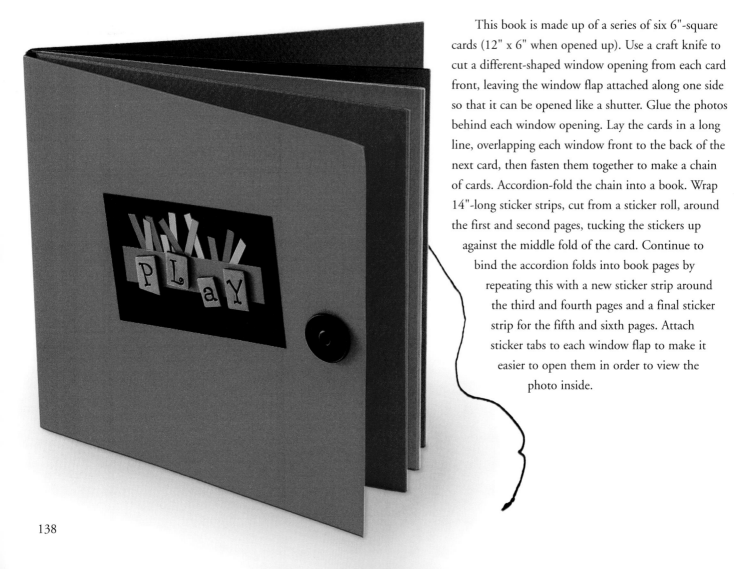

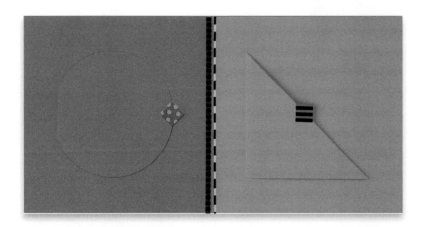

Sandi's Tip

When creating unusually shaped windows, place your photos behind each shape before building the book to ensure that your photos will work well behind each geometrically shaped opening.

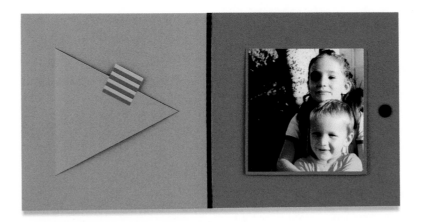

Acknowledgments

I want to thank the talented and helpful people at Chapelle, especially Lecia Monsen, my talented editor who is also a great listener, Rebecca Ittner, the photo stylist who not only styled the shots but also brought everything from food to flowers. I so appreciate the book designer, Matt Shay and Jo Packham who initiated this project.

I'd also like to thank so many friends whose photos grace some of the projects in this book, especially Becky Whaley-Butler and Kristy Bruce. And a huge thank-you to Laurie Weathersby who patiently helped me to navigate the foreign world of computers to convert my handwritten pages into a typed document.

I'd especially like to thank my good friend and mentor, Andrea Grossman, for giving me a creative home and more importantly, for inspiring me with her talent and her humanity.

Lastly I want to thank my family who are prominently featured in this book. I wouldn't be who I am without their support, inspiration, and sense of humor. I so appreciate my sister Diane, and niece Alyson, for delving into their shoe boxes and albums to share their photos with me. And most importantly, I'd like to thank my parents, Jess and Connie, who are at the heart of everything I do.

Resources

The supplies I used in the creation of my projects include the following:

3m Foam Adhesive:
• Adhesives

Canson:
• Paper

Chatterbox:
• Snaps

Clockits:
• Clock parts

E.K. Success:
• Paper punches
• Fibers

Ellison:
• Die-cuts
• Self-adhesive magnet
• Custom Dies

Fiskars:
• Punches
• Scissors

Glue Dots
• Adhesives

Hermafix
• Adhesives

Jewel Craft
• Colored wire

Jolee's Boutique
• 3-D embellishments

Kolo
• Albums

Making Memories:
• Magnetic rubber stamps
• Metal charms
• Rub-ons

Mrs. Grossman's:
• Albums
• Embossed cardstock
• Metal stickers
• Fabric stickers
• Stickers
• Vellum

Provo Craft
• Colored brads

Roll-a-Bind
• Binding System

Sakura Gold
• Silver and black pens

Sizzix:
• Die-cuts

The Paper Patch
• Patterned paper

Xyron
• Adhesives

Metric Equivalency Charts

inches to millimeters and centimeters

inches	mm	cm	inches	cm	inches	cm
1/8	3	0.3	9	22.9	30	76.2
1/4	6	0.6	10	25.4	31	78.7
1/2	13	1.3	12	30.5	33	83.8
5/8	16	1.6	13	33.0	34	86.4
3/4	19	1.9	14	35.6	35	88.9
7/8	22	2.2	15	38.1	36	91.4
1	25	2.5	16	40.6	37	94.0
1 1/4	32	3.2	17	43.2	38	96.5
1 1/2	38	3.8	18	45.7	39	99.1
1 3/4	44	4.4	19	48.3	40	101.6
2	51	5.1	20	50.8	41	104.1
2 1/2	64	6.4	21	53.3	42	106.7
3	76	7.6	22	55.9	43	109.2
3 1/2	89	8.9	23	58.4	44	111.8
4	102	10.2	24	61.0	45	114.3
4 1/2	114	11.4	25	63.5	46	116.8
5	127	12.7	26	66.0	47	119.4
6	152	15.2	27	68.6	48	121.9
7	178	17.8	28	71.1	49	124.5
8	203	20.3	29	73.7	50	127.0

yards to meters

yards	meters	yards	meters	yards	meters	yards	meters	yards	meters
1/8	0.11	2 1/8	1.94	4 1/8	3.77	6 1/8	5.60	8 1/8	7.43
1/8	0.11	2 1/8	1.94	4 1/8	3.77	6 1/8	5.60	8 1/8	7.43
1/4	0.23	2 1/4	2.06	4 1/4	3.89	6 1/4	5.72	8 1/4	7.54
3/8	0.34	2 3/8	2.17	4 3/8	4.00	6 3/8	5.83	8 3/8	7.66
5/8	0.46	2 1/2	2.29	4 1/2	4.11	6 1/2	5.94	8 1/2	7.77
5/8	0.57	2 5/8	2.40	4 5/8	4.23	6 5/8	6.06	8 5/8	7.89
3/4	0.69	2 3/4	2.51	4 3/4	4.34	6 3/4	6.17	8 3/4	8.00
7/8	0.80	2 7/8	2.63	4 7/8	4.46	6 7/8	6.29	8 7/8	8.12
1	0.91	3	2.74	5	4.57	7	6.40	9	8.23
1 1/4	1.03	3 1/4	2.86	5 1/8	4.69	7 1/4	6.52	9 1/8	8.34
1 1/4	1.14	3 1/4	2.97	5 1/4	4.80	7 1/4	6.63	9 1/4	8.46
1 3/8	1.26	3 3/8	3.09	5 3/8	4.91	7 3/8	6.74	9 3/8	8.57
1 1/2	1.37	3 1/2	3.20	5 1/2	5.03	7 1/2	6.86	9 1/2	8.69
1 5/8	1.49	3 5/8	3.31	5 5/8	5.14	7 5/8	6.97	9 5/8	8.80
1 3/4	1.60	3 3/4	3.43	5 3/4	5.26	7 3/4	7.09	9 3/4	8.92
1 7/8	1.71	3 7/8	3.54	5 7/8	5.37	7 7/8	7.20	9 7/8	9.03
2	1.83	4	3.66	6	5.49	8	7.32	10	9.14

Index

A

A Honeymoon to
   Remember 93–95
A Little about Mom & Dad ...46
A New Twist on Binding—
   Twist Ties 132–133
A Pail of A+ School
   Memories 26–29
A Spoonful of Memories—
   Favorite Family Foods ..62–65
About Sandi—
   Getting Personal 24–43
Acknowledgments 142

B

Birthday Blossoms for Dad ..49
Birthday Memories Are Popping
   Up—Phil's Birthday ...68–71

C

Canson 143
Cat Tales 38–39
Chatterbox 143
Childhood 10–11
Clockits 143

D

DIY 16

E

E.K. Success 143
Ellison 13, 143
Engaging
   Photos-in-a-box 82–85

F

Field of Dreams Baseball
   Diorama 102
Florida Photo Wall Art 105

For the Parents—Wedding Mini
   Book 72–73
Fun in the Sun Diorama 103

G

Glowing Memories—Photo
   Candles 81
Glue Dots 143
Graduating College
   & Teaching 12

H

Hanging Out with Photos—
   Vellum Room Divider 106
Heartfelt Thank-you Card ...107
Hermafix 143
Home 22–23

I

In the Beginning—Getting
   from There to Here 8
It's Elementary—Mike's School
   Photos 66
It's in the Can—
   Home Remodel 112–115
It's in the Cards— Christmas
   Cards Past 128–129

J

Jewel Craft 143
Jolee's Boutique 143

K

Kolo 143

M

Magnetic Bookmarks ..108–111
Making Memories 143

Making the Grade—Classroom
   Memories 76–80
Media Memories 34–37
Memorable Manhattan
   Meals 40–43
Metric Equivalency Charts ..143
Mother's Day Bouquet 48
Mrs. Grossman's 18, 143
My Friends 100–129
My Little Friends 130–141
My Mom & Dad 44–51
My Niece & Her Honey ..74–99
My Sister, Brother &
   Brother-in-law 52–73

N

Naval Aircraft Training 47
Nikon 19
Noteworthy Note Cards .116–117

R

Resources 143

S

Sandy Memories—Photos-on-
   a-stick 58
Save the Date
   Fridge Photos 86–87
Snappy Photos—
   Snap Bindings 136–137
Sneak-a-peek Mini Book—
   Sticker Binding 138–141
Snow Business Diorama ...104
Stretch Your Memories—
   Rubber-band Books .134–135
Studio 20–21

Studio & Home—Where It All
   Happens 20–23
Surprise Party 30–33

T

3M Foam Adhesive 143
Television 14
Thanks for the Memories .50–51
The Grass Is Greener 59
The Lovely Lindsay
   Baby Book 118–119
The Sky's the Limit—
   Skydiving 96–99
The Three Amigos 54–57
There's a New Baby in the Nest
   —Nesting Boxes 120–121
Thinking of You Card ..122–123
Timely Photos—
   Photo Clock 67
Tree-mendous Holiday
   Ornaments 60–61

V

Vacation Gift Album ...124–125
Wedding Keepsake Box ..88–92
Wedding Keepsake Box—
   Favor 92
Wedding Keepsake Box—
   Invitation 90
Wedding Keepsake Box—
   Program 91
Wedding Keepsake Box—
   Save-the-Date 89
Wonderful Wedding
   Guest Book 126–127